THE
WINES
IN THE
SUPER
MARKETS
2005

NED HALLEY

foulsham
LONDON • NEW YORK • TORONTO • SYDNEY

foulsham

The Publishing House, Bennetts Close, Cippenham, Slough, Berkshire, SL1 5AP, England

ISBN 0-572-03031-2

A CIP record for this book is available from the British Library

Printed in Italy

Contents

——A Personal Word——

This is an exclusive guide. It describes the wines on sale only in that clique of retailers formed by the supermarket chains. It is in these places that we buy three-quarters of all the wine we drink at home.

Each of the big chains sells several hundred different wines, and it is by no means easy to guess what an untried bottle might taste like or whether it will turn out to be good value for money. The point of this book is to give the reader some clues.

To make it as straightforward as possible, I have divided the book up according to the supermarkets themselves. Under each name, I have arranged the recommended wines first by colour, second by price range (up to £5 and above £5), and finally by country of origin – because that's the way the supermarkets arrange the wines on their shelves.

With very few exceptions, all the wines mentioned here are recommendations. I have a simple scoring system up to 10 points to indicate quality–value ratio (see the logic of my scoring system on page 15). Anything scoring 7 or above is, I believe, worth buying at the price shown.

This is an exclusive guide in another sense. It leaves out most of the very well known brands that are available in most, if not all, supermarkets. This does not mean I do not recommend Jacob's Creek, Ernest & Julio Gallo, Blossom Hill and so forth. It just means that I am not willing to fill the following pages with their eternally repeated names.

The wines that do get mentioned are, in the main, less well known. Many are the own-brands of the supermarkets in question. As many as I can find are from quirky individual growers who make wine in small quantities.

Admittedly, supermarkets are not famous for stocking wines produced on a very small scale. When you have 600 branches to supply and expectations of shifting every wine in large volume and fast, a couple of hundred cases of some rare vintage is not going to go very far. But some supermarkets do nevertheless include such wines among their faster-moving stock, and they are well worth seeking out.

Most of the wines in this book are in the price categories that account for most sales. About 88 per cent of wines sold for drinking at home cost under £5. About 18 per cent fall into the £4.50 to £6 bracket and a mere 4 per cent cost above £6.

Naturally, I believe most of the best wines are accounted for in that exclusive 4 per cent, and there are a good few of them in these pages. But the real point of this book is to recommend wines at prices that I – and you – know we're willing to pay.

The good news is that there is a lot of wine out there at affordable prices. Britain has the best choice of wine of any country in the world, and despite the monstrous taxation levied on it, it seems to me to be a luxury we can all afford – and a thoroughly healthy and civilising luxury at that.

I must apologise in advance for the inevitable fact that some of the wines I have recommended will have been discontinued or replaced with a new vintage, or will have increased (they rarely decrease) in price by the time you are reading this.

And I must reiterate the caveat that what I say about the wines and the retailers is based on my personal knowledge or understanding. Taste in all things is personal, and particularly so when it comes to wine. But I hope the impressions I have given of the hundreds of wines recommended in this guide will tempt you to try some new styles and flavours, and to look beyond all those beckoning brand names to the genuine, individual wines still clinging to their shelf space.

Introduction

The supermarkets have the take-home market for wine just about completely sewn up. Nearly eight bottles out of every ten are bought from multiples, and the traditional off-licence shops are having a relatively hard time of it.

I say 'relatively' because the wine business is booming, and this means that all kinds of retailers can benefit from the growth in wine drinking if they are any good. Sales of wine have increased by about 5 per cent in terms of value in the last year and are predicted to continue to grow at about this rate for years to come.

As the overall market expands, so does the top end. Nine out of ten bottles bought still cost under £5, but the proportion of wines bought costing between £4.50 and £6 is increasing.

This is to some extent due to the fact that wine prices in Britain are rising – something like 15 per cent over the last two years. The Chancellor of the Exchequer has contributed to this. Mr Brown's 2003 and 2004 budgets have added nearly 10 pence in duty and VAT per bottle over the two years. This has further incentivised cross-Channel 'booze cruising' and made it that much harder for retailers to maintain 'price points' from the endangered £2.99 bottle upwards.

But possibly the biggest factor in price increases is international currency fluctuation. Sterling has slipped about 15 per cent against the euro over the last couple of years, and this has certainly affected the price of our wine imports from the Continent. At the same time, however, the pound is holding up fairly well against the currencies of Australia, Latin America, South Africa and the US.

This may have some bearing on the fact that the domination of France and Italy in our wine market is now under such fierce assault. Australia has overtaken France on both quantity and value, and Italy in 2004 was finally displaced from third position by the US. South Africa is now snapping at Italy's heels, and it seems quite possible that before long New World wines will for the first time account for more than half of all UK sales.

Everyone wants a piece of the action, because Britain is the world's biggest importer of quality wines, and getting bigger every day. We drink about 1.2 billion bottles of wine a year – 20 bottles per head of population or, more relevantly, 40 bottles per head of the wine-drinking population (two-thirds of all adults, apparently). It sounds a lot, but it's still less per capita than in other northern European countries such as the Netherlands and Denmark, and less than half the consumption per capita in wine-producing countries including Italy and Portugal.

We have, in other words, a long way to go in terms of quantity. I hope, too, that we have a similar distance to travel in terms of quality and choice. As the British market 'matures' and more of us seek to trade up to more interesting wines, I sincerely hope the supermarkets will be there, expanding their ranges to tempt us.

The Choice

This book categorises the wines by nation of origin. This is largely to follow the system by which retailers arrange their wines, but also because it is the country or region of origin that still most distinguishes one style of wine from another. True, wines are now commonly labelled most prominently with their constituent grape variety, but to classify all the world's wines into the small number of principal grape varieties would make for categories of an unwieldy size.

Chardonnay and Sauvignon Blanc are overwhelmingly dominant among whites, and four grapes – Cabernet Sauvignon, Merlot, Shiraz and Tempranillo – account for a very high proportion of the red wines made worldwide.

But each area of production still – in spite of creeping globalisation – puts its own mark on its wines. Chardonnays from France remain (for the moment at least) quite distinct from those of Australia. Cabernet Sauvignon grown in a cool climate such as that of Bordeaux is a very different wine from Cabernet cultivated in the cauldron of the Barossa.

Of course there are 'styles' that winemakers worldwide seek to follow. Yellow, oaky Chardonnays of the type pioneered in South Australia are now made in South Africa, too – and in new, high-tech wineries in New Zealand and Chile, Spain and Italy. But the variety is still wide. Even though the 'upfront' high-alcohol wines of the New World have grabbed so much of the market, France continues to make the elegant wines it has always made in its classic regions. Germany still produces racy, delicate Rieslings; and the distinctive zones of Italy, Portugal and Spain make ever more characterful wines from indigenous grapes (as opposed to imported global varieties).

Among less expensive wines, the theme is, admittedly, very much a varietal one. The main selling point for most 'everyday' wines is the grape of origin rather than the country of origin. It makes sense, because the characteristics of various grape varieties do a great deal to identify taste. A bottle of white wine labelled 'Chardonnay' can reasonably be counted on to deliver that distinctive peachy or pineappley smell and soft, unctuous apple flavours. A Sauvignon Blanc should evoke gooseberries, green fruit and grassy freshness. And so on.

For all the domination of Chardonnay and Cabernet, there are plenty of other grape varieties making their presence felt. Argentina, for example, has revived the fortunes of several French and Italian varieties that had become near-extinct at home. And the grape that (in my view) can make the most exciting of white wines, the Riesling, is now doing great things in the southern hemisphere as well as at home in Germany.

The global varieties are, indeed, everywhere, but this book describes wines made from no fewer than 60 different grape varieties (see Glossary, starting on page 127), grown in every corner of the wine-making world. Let's hope this generous and growing choice is the shape of things to come.

The Price

How do retailers price their wines? Some bottles do seem inexplicably cheap, others unjustifiably expensive. But there is often a simple explanation. Big retailers work to price points. In wine, these are £2.99, £3.49, £3.99, even £9.99. You'll find very few bottles priced anywhere between these 50p spacings. A wine that wouldn't be profitable at £4.99 but would be at, say, £5.11, is priced at £5.49 in the hope that shoppers won't be wise to the fact that it is relatively poor value.

It's true that there are a few wines on supermarket shelves priced at £3.29, £3.79 etc. And 2004 has seen some supermarkets pass the Budget's 4p rise in excise duty directly on to the customer, just as they did, for a while, after a similar rise in 2003. When this book went to press, some of the consequent strange-looking prices ending in .03 pence were still force, but I suspect that in the long run the .99 will be reinstated, most likely at the expense of the producers.

But price can be a poor guide to quality even at the best of times. The only means by which any of us can determine a wine's value is by personal taste. The ideal bottle is one you like very much and would buy again at the same price without demur.

But just for curiosity's sake, it's fun to know what the wine itself actually costs, and what the retailer is making on it. The table on page 11 shows how the costs break down in a French wine costing £4.49 at a supermarket. This is a slightly unusual purchase by a supermarket, because the wine is being bought direct from the vineyard where it was made. Usually, retail multiples buy their wines by a less strenuous method, from agents and distributors in the UK.

Price paid by supermarket to supplier in France for the bottled wine	£1.40
Transport and insurance to UK	£0.28
Excise duty	£1.23
Cost to supermarket	£2.91
Supermarket's routine mark-up at 30%	£0.87
VAT at 17.5% on marked-up price	£0.66
Provisional shelf price	£4.44
Adjustment in price/VAT to price point	£0.05
Shelf price in supermarket	£4.49

The largest share of the money appears to go to the producer in France. But from his £1.40 he must pay the cost of growing and harvesting the grapes, pressing them, fermenting the juice, clarifying and treating the wine. Then he must bottle, cork, encapsulate, label and pack the wine into cartons. If his margin after these direct costs is 50p, he's doing well.

The prime profiteer, however, is not the supermarket, even though it makes a healthy 92p in mark-up. It is the Chancellor who does best, by miles. Excise duty and VAT are two of the cheapest taxes to collect, and from this single bottle of wine, the Treasury trousers a princely £1.89.

Travellers to wine-producing countries are always thrilled to find that by taking their own bottles, jugs or plastic casks to rustic vineyards offering wine on tap they can buy drinkable stuff for as little as 50p a litre. What too few travellers appreciate is that, for the wine itself, that's about what the supermarkets are paying for it. When enjoying your bargain bottle of wine, it is interesting to reflect on the economic reality known as 'added value' – which dictates that the worthiest person in the chain, the producer, has probably earned less than 10 per cent of the final price.

—Cork vs Screwcaps—

On the morning I set out for the cork forests of Portugal, an announcement arrived in the post from a top New Zealand wine company, headlined: 'Villa Maria Says Screw Corks'.

Villa Maria's owner, George Fistonich, is refusing to sell any more wine in bottles with corks. 'We are 100 per cent committed to the quality that the use of screwcap closures guarantees,' he declares: 'To achieve this, Villa Maria has had to inform distributors that it is screw caps or nothing. This may seem a little harsh, but no other industry in the world accepts the type of product failure experienced using cork.'

Reading this at the airport, waiting for the plane to Lisbon, I began to wonder if Mr Fistonich might be objecting just a little too strongly. True, we have all heard of 'corked' wine, but after centuries of happily confining wine in bottles with nothing else, is the cork really dead?

There are plenty of winemakers, and retailers, who think so. One in ten bottles now has either a plastic stopper or a screwcap. This is due to a recent surge in the number of wines spoiled by a taint known as 2,4,6 trichloroanisole, or TCA, which imparts an unpleasant, musty aroma and flavour – and has been blamed on the cork manufacturers.

And so to Portugal, where the country's – and the world's biggest cork producer, Amorim, has invited me to see for myself what is being done about this problem. I am met by Carlos de Jesus, Amorim's marketing director, who conducts me to the cork oak forests, an hour's drive northeast of Lisbon and extending over hundreds of square kilometres beyond. It's the harvest, and highly skilled men armed with light, broad-bladed axes are stripping the trunks and lower branches of the trees of their bark, in sections up to 5 centimetres thick and a metre or more long. The process takes place once every nine years.

'It's like a face peel in beauty treatment,' says Carlos. 'It leaves the skin a little tender, but renewed. We harvest between May and August, when growth is at its most active. The first harvest is after 25 years. It does the trees no harm. They live up to 200 years.'

This is obviously the most natural and renewable means of providing the raw material for bottle stoppers. And I do wonder how the wine industry could ever have adopted cork-shaped stoppers made from what Carlos calls 'oil-derived products' instead. But plastic 'corks' look doomed. They can be difficult to extract and hard to unwind from the corkscrew. It's impossible to push them back into the bottle. They utterly lack the indispensable elasticity of natural cork.

It is the screwcap that is the only real long-term rival for cork. It obviates the corkscrew, and may, in time, prove to be as good at preserving the wine in healthy condition, as well as being proof against tainted flavour.

Back in the forest, we next visit a huge Amorim plant where the peeled bark is stacked in endless canyons several metres high, before being boiled in newly installed vats incorporating a continuous water-filtering system to remove impurities and combat the dreaded taint.

'In the last two and a half years we have spent $43 million on re-equipping to fight TCA,' says Carlos. It's a candid admission that the infection has been a problem for this major industry employing 20,000 people in Portugal.

Extensive research suggests that the taint has become more common due to chemical reactions with chlorine products used in the wine industry. But Carlos is quick to point out that TCA does not affect only cork. 'It can adhere to wood, to concrete, to metal and to plastic – including oil-derived stoppers and screwcaps too,' he says, reminding us of the winery in the US that lately traced the TCA in its wine to an infection not in its corks but in its drainage system. The infection was so severe the entire plant had to be closed.

The task at Amorim is to ensure that all the three billion corks they produce annually are TCA free. And they are succeeding. In the last year, sales of their Twin Top cork, formed by a disc of whole cork at either end of a cylinder of agglomerated cork granules, have passed 800 million – and there has been a complaint about only one of them.

It's down to changed practices in the company's dozen production centres, including a new steam-treatment system, specifically developed to counter TCA, through which every single cork passes. The company has also installed gas chromatography equipment to detect any infections.

I was greatly impressed with what Amorim have achieved to restore the good name of its own corks, if not the many more that are made by other producers around the world. But can Amorim hope that these heroic efforts will impress winemakers such as George Fistonich?

Antonio Amorim, chairman of the 133-year-old company, acknowledges that views have become polarised. 'In Europe, cork and wine is an old marriage. It's accepted,' he told me. 'But in the New World they question everything and I don't blame them for that.'

He acknowledges that his own industry was slow to respond to the TCA crisis in the 1990s, when the wine trade started to blame every duff bottle on TCA-affected corks, even though cork was really only responsible for a fraction of the total. 'Six or seven years ago in this industry we could only talk philosophy, but now we can talk science,' he says. 'TCA is a problem we feel we have solved, although I would never claim to have eradicated it. But now we can start to speak about the many positive aspects of cork – how it contributes to the good of wine, to its health and development.'

He seems calmly confident, and is prepared for a long campaign. 'We are patient people,' he says. 'After all, we wait 25 years to collect our first harvest, and we are prepared to take time to convince consumers that this natural product is the best one for now and for the future.'

The Supermarket Best Wine Buys

First, a short explanation of my scoring system. As an entirely subjective guide to relative value among the wines mentioned in the book, I use a scoring scale of 0 to 10. In the notes I took while tasting, I gave each wine a score within this range, and just about all the wines that were given a score of 7 and above are included. Wines scoring 6 and under are mostly left out, because this is not a book in which there is space to decry wines I have not liked.

I would recommend any of the wines with a score of 7 or above. Those scoring 7 are those I account good wines at a fair price. A score of 8 signifies a very good wine at a fair price and a score of 9 indicates special quality and value. Those that earn 10 out of 10 are, obviously enough, the wines I don't think can be bettered.

Out of the hundreds I have tasted, just 32 wines scored the maximum 10 out of 10 on my personal scale. They are listed overleaf in ascending price order. A good number of them are very inexpensive and are rated so highly because they seemed to me quite remarkable value for money. It might be of interest to point out that the number of top scores was highest from Waitrose, with eight; followed by six from Majestic; and four from Sainsbury's, Somerfield and Tesco. Countries of origin are led by France, with seven top scores; Germany and Spain, with four; Australia with three; and Argentina, Italy, New Zealand and South Africa, with two each. Only one each for Hungary and the United States.

My Top Supermarket Wines

Red Wines

£5.49   Château Villepreux 2002   Waitrose

£6.49   Côtes du Rhône Villages Sablet,
        Domaine de Piaugier, 2001   Majestic

£6.99   Wolvenbosch Family Vineyards
        Shiraz 2002   Marks & Spencer

£6.99   Diemersfontein Pinotage 2003   Waitrose

£9.99   Valpolicella Classico Superiore Ripasso
        la Cassetto di Ettore Righetti 2000   Majestic

Pink Wine

£5.49   Torres San Medin Cabernet Sauvignon
        Rosé 2003   Sainsbury's

White Wines

£5.99   Lindemans Coonawarra Botrytis
        Riesling 1999   Somerfield

£7.49   Finest Marlborough Sauvignon Blanc 2003   Tesco

£7.99   Kaituna Hills Reserve Sauvignon
        Blanc 2003   Marks & Spencer

£8.49   Jordan Estate Chardonnay 2003   Booths

£11.99 Rully 1er Cru Vielles Vignes Vincent
        Girardin 2002   Majestic

Fortified Wines

£5.04   Finest Oloroso Sherry   Tesco

£5.99   Solera Jerezana Dry Amontillado Sherry   Waitrose

£5.99   Solera Jerezana Dry Oloroso Sherry   Waitrose

£6.49   Hidalgo La Gitana Manzanilla Sherry   Majestic,
                                            Sainsbury's, Waitrose

Aldi

This German chain has more supermarkets than any of the others appearing in this book – 5,000 of them, across Europe, including 250 in the UK. The 'no-frills' chains are a source of genuine wine bargains. Unlike most of these stores, however, Aldi has its own range of wines – some of them rather grand – and prices are quite remarkably low.

The half-dozen classic clarets mentioned here are inevitably in short supply, but well worth keeping an eye out for, as they are remarkable bargains, with the common very minor drawback that they all need to be stored for a couple of years or more to reach their ideal maturity for drinking. Otherwise, all those I have scored as 9 would have been marked 10.

If you don't know where your nearest Aldi is, ring the Store Location Line on 08705 134262 or look on the web at **www.aldi-stores.co.uk**.

RED WINES   UNDER £5

ARGENTINA

7 **Hacienda San José Malbec 2001**   £3.99
Soft, easy, mature, dense wine with a briary style.

AUSTRALIA

8 **Mayrah Estates Cabernet Sauvignon**   £3.49
Light but well put together Aussie Cabernet at the lowest
price imaginable. More like a European wine, and none
the worse for that.

7 **Evolution Old Vine Shiraz**   £3.99
Straight, non-vintage, easy-drinking bargain red.

7 **Ransome's Vale Shiraz Petit Verdot**   £3.99
Distinctly jammy, berry-style bargain red balanced with
good, gripping dry finish.

FRANCE

9 **Château Selection Claret**
Patrice Calvet 2002   £2.99
Ripe and fully formed claret at an unheard-of price is a
real pleasure to drink and well presented.

8 **Chemin des Papes**
Côtes du Rhône 2002   £3.29
Light and spicy CDR in a very fancy pot-shaped bottle is
laughably cheap at this price.

SPAIN

9 Viña Decaña Crianza 2000 £2.99
Amazing quality at the price from this mature-tasting, Rioja-style, dry-finishing, deep, smooth and satisfying red from Utiel-Requena region.

9 Bella Viña Vino de Mesa £2.29
Ever such a humble Spanish 'table wine', but it's got spice and warmth in its bright, clean flavour.

RED WINES £5 PLUS

FRANCE

9 Château Vieux Rivière,
Lalande de Pomerol 1999 £6.99
Middling in weight, but hefty with blackberry-fruit and with the classic cedary notes of the best claret, and seriously underpriced.

9 Olivier du Château Olivier,
Pessac Léognan 2000 £6.99
'Second wine' of famed Chateau Olivier. A coal-dark young claret with classic aromas of violets and mint and intense, pure fruit, with the balance between richness and dryness unique to the best reds of Bordeaux. Fantastic wine to drink now if you decant it an hour or two in advance, or keep several years to allow it to evolve to sublime maturity.

9 Château Capet Guillier,
St Emilion Grand Cru 2000 £6.99
Needs keeping a year or two, but already showing the signs of a very good claret – rich, dark ripeness and huge concentration, with lush fruit currently camouflaged by liquorice tannins. The 2000 vintage is a great one, and much sought after, so wine of this status won't be around much longer.

FRANCE

9 Château Merissac St Emilion 2000 £8.99
Classic cigar box and pure elegant blackcurrant-fruit
from a great vintage that is already mellow, supple and
long – but it really should be given another couple of
years.

9 S de Château Siran 2001 £8.99
'Second wine' of famed Margaux estate is fabulous, if
still a bit young, and evidently destined to be a silky,
balanced classic.

8 La Closerie de Malescasse Haut
Médoc 2001 £8.99
Purply but already approachable young claret that will
develop well.

WHITE WINES	UNDER £5

ARGENTINA

9 Hacienda San José Sauvignon Blanc 2003 £3.99
Notably lively and zesty grassy-gooseberry Sauvignon of
inspiring quality.

GERMANY

9 Niersteiner Gutes Domtal Spätlese £2.49
This comes in a sapphire-blue bottle and looks fun. It
tastes pretty good, too, with a nice apple-blossom bloom
and soft but crisp-finishing fruit that will appeal to
many. The price is simply unbelievable, but Aldi, being a
German company with more stores across Europe than
all our Big Four supermarket chains put together,
presumably has immense buying power on its home
territory. I hope they will stock more and more German
wines.

ITALY

8 **Pinot Grigio Villa Malizia 2003**   £3.99
Lush, almost tropical, dry white of real interest, with melon-ripe fruit and eager clean finish.

WHITE WINES	£5 PLUS

FRANCE

9 **Philippe Michel Crémant du Jura**
   Chardonnay Brut 2001   £5.49
Handsomely presented vintage from Alpine France has gentle fizz – crémant means 'creaming', as distinct from the more vigorous sparkle of, say, champagne – and generous, yeasty-appley, dry but full Chardonnay fruit. This is very cheap but looks and tastes classy – a decided improvement on most Spanish cava.

Asda

I was thrilled to be honoured with an invitation to taste the wines of Asda this year – the first time in a long while. And it was worth turning up, because there are all sorts of wines here, particularly from the southern hemisphere, that I have not seen elsewhere.

As ever, Asda have a uniquely random-looking collection of prices, none of which seem to end in .99. This may be a mere tactic in what is presumably a perpetual battle between supermarket giants to differentiate themselves when so much of what they sell is the same, but on the whole I think Asda's prices are genuinely a wee bit lower than those of rival chains.

It's a huge wine range, but please note that some of the grander items that appear in the following pages are on sale only in the largest branches.

RED WINES   UNDER £5

AUSTRALIA

`9` **Wolf Blass Eaglehawk Cabernet 2002**   £4.48
Gripping and generous, peppery-cassis, rounded mid-weight red of real character at this relatively modest price.

`8` **Asda Australian Cabernet Shiraz**   £3.78
Budget non-vintage blend is brambly and fun with clean finish.

`8` **Bear Crossing Cabernet-Shiraz 2002**   £4.01
'Up-front' – but not overbearing, one might say – blend from Angove's is sunny and ripe, and raises funds for saving the dear little koala.

ITALY

`9` **Asda Valpolicella 2003**   £2.98
A very pleasant surprise, this charming cherry-fruit lightweight (11.5% alcohol) from a DOC that generally disappoints. The fruit is well knit and complete, and dances on the tongue, finishing properly brisk and dry.

`8` **Asda Chianti Classico 2002**   £4.98
The price is a lure, because Chianti has become generally so expensive, but this is a good one in its own right, with likable austerity, cherry perfume and recognisable style.

`7` **Asda Valpolicella Classico 2002**   £4.98
Darker wine than the flighty thing above, and with a different sort of appeal. Less distinctive.

PORTUGAL

`8` **Hearty Red**   £4.02
No-nonsense agricultural plonk with plenty of grunt has just a shade of that minty Portuguese darkness. Good stuff.

S AFRICA

9   **Asda South African Pinotage 2003**   £3.22
Purply, even lurid, colour and a big sweet nose, but this is a genuine wine, naturally ripe and not over-done, though 14% alcohol, and good value.

9   **Asda South African Merlot 2003**   £3.32
Well formed legitimate black fruit Merlot with real appeal, especially at this knockdown price.

SPAIN

8   **Asda Tempranillo**   £3.00
Straight non-vintage varietal from Estremadura has sweet strawberry nose, corresponding fruit and cheery juiciness.

8   **Asda Marques del Norte Rioja**   £3.35
A very cheap Rioja from a mix of vintages and unoaked to make a pleasingly perfumed light red of recognisable style.

TUNISIA

7   **Sirocco Cabernet Syrah 2000**   £4.98
Bright maroon colour and plenty of hot-climate bramble on the nose, it's slightly woody but drinkable plonk that scores for ethnicity, I suppose.

RED WINES   £5 PLUS

AUSTRALIA

9   **Penmara Five Families Pinot Noir 2002**   £5.98
Quite pale in colour and with a sweet strawberry nose, this well priced wine delivers a burst of fruit in the mouth – a really bright-tasting wine with 14% alcohol.

9   Serafino Shiraz 2000   £6.11

Deep purply colour and a combination of juiciness with a dark, chocolate inner flavour bring an Italian style to this dry-finishing pasta matcher with 14.5% alcohol.

8   Nepenthe Tryst Red 2003   £6.61

Briary berry-fruit red with zingy liveliness, summery ripeness and 14% alcohol. Screwcap.

8   Hanging Rock Kilfara Pinot Noir 2002   £7.98

Light in colour but generous in cherry-strawberry fruit, this is a nice gamey Pinot with an appreciable grip on the tastebuds. Screwcap.

8   Serafino Shiraz Reserve 2001   £8.98

Smoothed-out, extravagant, warmly peppery black-fruit special-occasion red worth the money.

8   Rock Red Shiraz Grenache Pinot 2002   £5.92

With its odd mix of constituent grapes, this seems tailor-made for the indecisive drinker, and it even has recognisable characteristics of all three varieties. Fun wine that needs a meaty dish.

AUSTRALIA

9   Asda Chianti Classico Riserva 2001   £6.98

Very nice one from giant producer Cecchi has dense colour, squished blackberry nose and a dark heart with a flicker of richness. A really good Chianti for the money.

ITALY

8   Asda Marques del Norte
Rioja Reserva 1998   £6.98

Rich colour to a mature vanilla-oaked Rioja in which the fruit is nevertheless long, lively and lush.

SPAIN

PINK WINES — UNDER £5

AUSTRALIA

9 **Mighty Murray Rosé 2003** £3.77

Colour is close to pale red, but the wine has an acidity like a brisk white – in between these poles this is a really smashing pink, distinctly of its own style and cheap for what it is.

FRANCE

8 **Roquemartin Côtes de Provence Rosé 2003** £4.98

Odd amphora-shaped bottle, but otherwise a straightforward, excellent pale-salmon, elegantly dry and briskly strawberry-fruit pink of real character.

7 **Asda Rosé d'Anjou** £2.81

Pale salmon colour and a boiled-sweet whiff, but a fruity off-dry glugger with plenty of pinkness for your pound.

PINK WINES — £5 PLUS

USA

9 **Fetzer Valley Oaks Syrah Rosé 2003** £6.02

This is as good as rosé needs to get. Shocking pink colour, a perky, fleshy wine that shines with the flavours of summer fruit. Well worth paying the extra for. Screwcap.

WHITE WINES — UNDER £5

AUSTRALIA

8 **Bear Crossing Semillon Chardonnay 2003** £4.01

Well coloured tropical-aroma wine with straight peachy Chardonnay fruit dominant.

AUSTRALIA

8 **Wolf Blass Eaglehawk Chardonnay 2003** **£4.48**
Pleasing gold colour, and flavour, with an equally pleasing balance of richness and minerality.

CHILE

9 **Chilean Reserve Sauvignon Blanc 2003** **£4.48**
Cracking crisp, well coloured and zingy-grassy Sauvignon of real character with long-lasting flavour and a super citrus finish.

8 **Asda Chilean Chardonnay 2003** **£2.97**
A softened style but not an enfeebled one, this is a very respectable apple-fresh Chardonnay for the money.

FRANCE

9 **Paul Mas Sauvignon Blanc** **£4.98**
A well coloured, superbly fresh and lively vin de pays d'Oc that is elegant in its restraint but vivaciously fruity.

HUNGARY

8 **Asda Hungarian Dry Chardonnay 2003** **£2.81**
Very cheap but perfectly fresh and legitimate glugger without any fatal flaws.

8 **Asda Hungarian Medium
Chardonnay 2003** **£2.81**
Quite distinct from the dry version above, I'm sure this is more than just a sugared edition of same! It tastes riper and softer, off-dry, and not unpleasant. Terrible old-fashioned label which surely won't aid sales, even at this price.

ITALY

8 **Asda Pinot Grigio Del Trentino 2003** **£4.98**
Good herbaceous dry wine with length and plenty of dimension from sub-Alpine Italy, where most of the nation's best whites come from.

ITALY

🍷**7** **Asda Pinot Grigio del Venezia 2003**   £4.00
Clean, crisp PG with more smoky character than most in this price bracket.

SPAIN

🍷**9** **Torres Viña Sol 2003**   £4.38
Cracking new vintage of this constant dry white from Spain's best winemaker, Miguel Torres. It's wholly un-Spanish, in an aromatic style reminiscent of the best kind of Alsace Pinot Blanc, as sunny and refreshing as it sounds. Screwcap.

USA

🍷**7** **Pacific Bay Chardonnay
Pinot Grigio 2003**   £4.94
Slightly steely dry white from Fetzer of California is sunny and zesty.

WHITE WINES	£5 PLUS

AUSTRALIA

🍷**8** **Serafino Chardonnay 2003**   £6.01
Nice top note of sweet apple on this triangularly flavoured midweight dry wine.

🍷**8** **Nepenthe Tryst White 2003**   £6.61
Zippy Sauvignon Blanc nose on a lively dry white packed with interesting flavours of grassiness and gentle sweetness. Screwcap.

🍷**8** **Asda Chablis 1er Cru 2002**   £9.57
Fine flinty young wine with a hint of the 'Côte d'Or' rich style of more southerly burgundy.

Booths

Booths is tiny by supermarket-chain standards, with a total of just 25 branches, all of them in the north-west of England. But the company has earned a deservedly elevated reputation for its range of wines, and these are available to shoppers nationwide via mail order. There is a very well-presented website at **www.boothswine.co.uk** or you can telephone 0800 197 0066 for a mail order list and to place orders. The company also has a remarkable online operation offering more than 20,000 different wines, with the apposite website name of **www.everywine.co.uk**.

The wines here are from the considerable range stocked in the stores and available by mail order. Many of the wines are unique to Booths, and there is no doubt that the company, which is still family-owned, punches well above its weight in this competitive field.

RED WINES   UNDER £5

FRANCE

8 **Louis Chatel Rouge Listel 2002**   £2.99
Leafy-smelling bargain vin de pays d'Oc has friendly briary flavours and no obvious faults.

8 **Château Cluzan 2001**   £4.99
Consolingly dark and dense claret with good chewy fruit and brisk blackcurrant highlights – one of many 'ordinary' red Bordeaux of unexpected substance tasted during the year.

7 **Syrah Domaine du Petit Roubié 2002**   £4.29
Organic vin de pays de l'Hérault has a green-fruit whiff but is ripe enough in the flavour, with grip and structure.

ITALY

8 **Barocco Rosso del Salento 2002**   £3.49
Surprisingly light for a red from the scorched-earth far south of Italy, but there's no lack of fruit and firmness of flavour.

PORTUGAL

7 **Portada 2003**   £3.99
Curious Estremadura red used to be plumper and longer in flavour than this, but still has the same unusual and agreeable cinnamon and clove notes in the dark fruit. Smart new packaging and higher price to match.

SPAIN

8 **Escobera Jumilla 2002**   £4.99
Raisiny, peppery heavyweight just short of overripe to enjoy with winter stews.

USA

8 **Fetzer Pacific Bay Merlot 2002**   £4.99
Lovely black cherry nose on this Californian glugger, followed up by lively squashy fruit.

RED WINES   £5 PLUS

ARGENTINA

🍷8 **La Remonta Malbec 2002**   £5.99
Familiar whiff of leather in the smell, but the fruit is
really quite yielding and soft – classy wine.

AUSTRALIA

🍷9 **Bleasdale Shiraz Cabernet 2002**   £6.99
Real smoothie with a caramel note in the nose and silk
in the texture as well as plenty of ripeness, 14% alcohol
and a beguiling aftertaste.

🍷8 **Novello Nero 2002**   £5.99
Yes, it's Australian, but mostly comprising Italian grapes
Barbera and Sangiovese. Fresh green-leaf notes in the
aroma and nice roasty fruit with brisk finish – and 14%
alcohol.

🍷8 **Peter Lehmann Clancy's Red 2002**   £6.99
Light touch to this pure and rather sleek Barossa blend.

🍷8 **Brown Brothers Graciano 2001**   £7.99
Italian-style red with special appeal in its well-contrived
weight and balance. Sleek but strong at 14% alcohol.

🍷8 **High Trellis Cabernet Sauvignon
     D'Arenberg 2001**   £8.49
Juicy but cerebral balanced pure-fruit red from a famous
McLaren Vale vineyard, justifying its price.

🍷8 **Skillogalee Shiraz 2000**   £12.99
Very dark and intense minty-spicy Clare Valley wine is as
dark in flavour as in appearance – emphatically
delicious.

CHILE

7 **Casa Lapostolle Cabernet Sauvignon 2001** £6.99
On the whole, I'm a Casa Lapostolle fan, and this young, gripping brambly red is OK, but a bit pricy.

9 **Château Pierrail 2001** £5.99
Holy grail stuff, this – good, affordable claret. This humble Bordeaux Supérieur is inky dark and with a wafting, Aussie-style nose; dense black Merlot fruit is similarly generous, but it has the keynote elegant balance of the real thing. Good now and will improve for at least a couple of years.

9 **Rasteau Domaine des Coteaux
de Travers 2002** £6.99
Chunky-spicy ripe Rhône village wine with gripping edge of flavour and dark heart. Very good wine from what was a difficult vintage.

FRANCE

8 **Chorey les Beaune Beaumonts Nicolas Potel
2000** £12.99
Good show-off wine to take to a foodie dinner party. Lovely cherry-strawberry Pinot Noir of classic character from a good grower in a famed appellation, and mature, too.

8 **St Aubin 1er Cru Derrière la Tour
Domaine Bachelet 2000** £11.99
Almost rosé-pale, this delicate, mature burgundy is earthy, sunny and layered – it will please devotees of the genre.

8 **Faugères Domaine Gilbert Alquier 2000** £7.99
Expensive for the humble Languedoc AC of Faugères, but this is a splendidly mature and structured black-fruit wine with relishable notes of prune, spice and other goodies.

FRANCE

8 **Chinon Cuvée de Pacques Domaine de la Roche Honneur 2003**   £5.49

Authentic green-fruit Loire red with genuinely refreshing, palate-stimulating flavours. It's good to see such a good example of this increasingly elusive wine on sale.

7 **Domaine Chaume-Arnaud Côtes du Rhône Villages Vinsobres 2001**   £7.99

Pale but gripping peppery wine of character.

ITALY

10 **Concerto Lambrusco Reggiano Medici Ermete 2002**   £6.49

This is the Lambrusco of old, the real thing, in a champagne-type bottle, very dark and dry and foamy rather than fizzy. It's the most deliciously refreshing briary red wine imaginable. Drink chilled, with or without food.

9 **Rosso di Montalcino Azienda Agricola Poliziano 2002**   £7.99

Rich, inviting nose on this Tuscan giant, and lashings of vivid, creamy, brambly fruit, with a rewarding clean finish. Long-living wine already very good to drink – and so deliciously Italian.

8 **Salice Salenino Agricole Vallone 2000**   £5.49

Burnt-orange oxidised-looking colour and a corresponding burnt-rubber note to the dark flavour, but this is a good, fun, mature wine that will go well with salami.

8 **Bardolino Azienda Agricola Cavalhina 2003**   £5.99

With more weight than the usual weedy stuff from Bardolino, this is a breezy cherry-red to drink cool.

8   Merloblu Castello di Luzzano 2002   £5.59

Slightly tough first flavour, but this delivers a real gush of underlyingly yielding, sweet-black Merlot fruit with a roasted note – great with red meats.

8   Archidamo Primitivo Di Manduria Pervini 2001   £6.99

Strong (14% alcohol) tannic red suggesting sun-baked fruit and a hint of brimstone, but I liked it a lot – needs a meaty dish with it.

8   Hochar Red 2000   £6.99

Pale, fading red with petrolly, spicy, briary flavours that assemble into a fascinating and exotic dry red, a bit reminiscent of some kinds of very old claret. Typical of the style of Serge Hochar's much-loved Château Musar in the former Lebanese war zone, and a real talking point.

9   Wither Hills Pinot Noir 2002   £13.99

This is one of the great Kiwi reds. It's an unusually rustic, earthy style for New Zealand, really quite Burgundian, and quite fabulously delicious, too. I even like the radical-chic naff label.

8   Quinta de la Rosa Douro Tinto 2001   £8.99

Lush porty red with silk and mint in the dark, dark flavours.

ITALY

LEBANON

NEW ZEALAND

PORTUGAL

S AFRICA

9 Firefinch What the Birds Left
Ripe Red 2002   £5.99
Blackberry aromas fairly fly off this big, generous Cape
wine which is miles better than might be expected from
the silly, verbose label – a long, lush gripper and 14%
alcohol.

9 Springfield Estate Cabernet
Sauvignon 2001   £8.99
Wildly blackcurrant nose and deliciously rounded out
cassis fruit in this beguiling, pure-silk red – a super-
league Cabernet.

SPAIN

9 Mas Collet Celler de Capçanes 2001   £5.99
Cassis syrup smell to this very dark, oaked red is
followed up by a balanced fruit of elegant weight. Great
stuff and cheaper than elsewhere.

8 Inurrieta Tinto Norte Navarra 2002   £5.99
Cabernet-Merlot blend has a fruitful minty outcome –
untypical of the region, but a pleasing juicy wine.

8 Pesquera Crianza Ribera del Duero Bodega
Alejandro Fernandez 2001   £11.99
Rich, minty, dark red of luxurious intensity and with a
real rush of cassis fruit.

PINK WINES	UNDER £5

FRANCE

8 Bellefontaine Syrah Rosé 2003   £3.99
Pale blossom colour and plenty of brisk flavour in this
affordable vin de pays d'Oc.

8   **Château Lamothe-Vincent Rosé 2003**   **£4.49**
Brightly coloured Bordeaux pink has blackcurrant nose and fresh briary-sweet fruit. Quite a mouth-filler for the money.

FRANCE

PINK WINES	£5 PLUS

8   **Bardolino Chiaretto Azienda Agricola Cavalchina 2003**   **£5.49**
Much red Bardolino looks pale enough to be rosé, but this is a real rosé in its own right, and not without its attractions – fresh and brisk to drink with summery food.

ITALY

WHITE WINES	UNDER £5

9   **Bellefontaine Chardonnay 2002**   **£3.89**
Super-ripe vin de pays d'Oc is heavy with sunny fruit – and light on price.

8   **Château Lamothe-Vincent 2003**   **£3.99**
Well coloured, dry white Bordeaux has a pleasing vegetal scent and lots of fresh gooseberry-pineapple flavour.

FRANCE

8   **Inycon Fiano 2003**   **£4.99**
Yellow, oxidised-style, almost sherry-like dry white from Sicily is intriguing and rather delicious to drink with seafood.

ITALY

8   **Peaks View Sauvignon Blanc 2003**   **£3.99**
Grapefruit and other interesting items evident on the nose of this lively Sauvignon, followed up by corresponding flavours and soft finish.

S AFRICA

SPAIN

8 **Castillo de Maluenda Bianco Bodegas
y Vinedos del Jalon 2003**   £3.29
Soft, grapy dry wine with convincingly complete flavour
at such a low price.

WHITE WINES   £5 PLUS

9 **Yalumba Y Series Viognier 2003**   £6.99
Barossa variation on the endless Viognier theme has
heaps of fruit, characterised by flavours of blanched
almonds and preserved fruit, and is made special by the
crispest of limey finishes. Great stuff.

8 **Peter Lehmann Semillon 2002**   £5.49
Banana, pineapple and other Semillon signatures in this
fresh, flowery dry white. Screwcap.

8 **Bleasdale Verdelho 2002**   £7.49
Intriguing fino sherry-like depths in a tangy but complex
dry wine with a citrus twang at the finish.

8 **Hermit Crab Marsanne Viognier
D'Arenberg Vineyards 2003**   £7.99
Vanilla and spice are in the mix of this fleshily fruity yet
dry finishing and distinctive item. Lots of interest for the
money. Screwcap.

8 **Skillogalee Riesling 2003**   £9.99
Bracing tangy-limey Clare Valley wine of great
concentration to go with white meat dishes.

AUSTRALIA

CHILE

8 Casa Lapostolle Chardonnay 2002 £6.49
Gold colour translates into an opulently flavoured
creamy-oaky, spearmint-tinged grand dry white of real
class and 14% alcohol.

7 Concha y Toro Trio
Sauvignon Blanc 2003 £5.99
At last, Chilean Sauvignon is starting to take off. This
one is impressively brisk and crisp with lush grassy fruit.

ENGLAND

8 Curious Grape Schonburger 2002 £6.99
A grapey aromatic off-dry wine, this also has freshness
and vigour. Revealingly good English wine.

FRANCE

8 Flambeau d'Alsace Hugel 2002 £5.99
A basketful of spicy, smoky, herbaceous flavours in this
'edelzwicker' wine blended from all the noble grape
varieties of Alsace.

8 Attitude Sauvignon Blanc, Pascal Jolivet
2003 £6.99
Irritating name but a generously fruity Loire vin de pays
of indisputable quality.

8 Mas de Daumas Gassac Blanc 2003 £13.99
From a famed and spirallingly expensive Languedoc
estate, this grand dry white from a mélange of grapes
including Viognier and Chardonnay is a beguiling
conversation piece.

8 Chablis 1er Cru Les Lys, Daniel Defaix
1998 £15.99
You pay for maturity when buying top-flight Chablis,
and this golden-delicious item is worth the investment.

GERMANY

8 **Rudesheimer Magdalenenkreuz Riesling Spätlese Joseph Leitz 2002** £9.99

Classic core of ripe, lush, apple-crisp Riesling fruit in this racy, Rhine late-harvest wine at 9% alcohol – thrilling stuff.

ITALY

8 **Verdicchio dei Castelli di Jesi Classico Azienda Santa Barbara 2003** £8.99

You don't see much of this touristy Italian white in this sort of price bracket, but it's quite delicious, sweetly ripe and grapy but overall quite dry and very refreshing – an outstandingly interesting rarity, namely Italian white wine that isn't boring.

NEW ZEALAND

9 **Jackson Estate Sauvignon Blanc 2003** £8.49

Excitingly vivid grassy-asparagussy complex-flavoured Sauvignon that's outstanding even by Kiwi standards.

9 **Kim Crawford Riesling 2003** £8.59

Lively limey lush and stirringly flavoursome mineral wine. Screwcap.

S AFRICA

10 **Jordan Estate Chardonnay 2003** £8.49

There's a madly extravagant style to this perennial classic never fails to leave me feeling uplifted. It's a pure-fruit, sultry-ripe, toffee-suggesting, perfectly weighted wine (14% alcohol) that I believe is unmatched anywhere at this price.

SPAIN

8 **Albariño Pazo de Senorans 2003** £8.99

From the admired region of Rias Baixas, a complex and dimensional dry white of great freshness.

Co-op

The Co-op can hardly lay claim to the most pretentious image, but the wines in the 2,000 or so licensed convenience stores and larger outlets are very well chosen.

Even in small Co-op branches you will find a decent choice of real quality wines, and in the 'superstores' the selection will run into hundreds of different lines.

A feature of all the own-brand wines is their back labels. It is the Co-op's policy to state all the ingredients in their own wines, and the back labels look very busy on account of it. Co-op Australian Merlot, for example, boasts this ingredient list: 'Grapes. Tartaric acid, Tannin, Preservative (Sulphur Dioxide). Made using: Yeast, Yeast Nutrient (Diammonium phosphate), Copper sulphate, Carbon dioxide, Nitrogen. Cleared using: Filtration, Gelatine, Pectinolytic enzymes.'

Nothing sinister here, I promise, and in an ingredient-conscious world, the Co-op should be congratulated on its openness. No other supermarket – and no other wine retailer, including organic wine specialists – is similarly upfront, and I hope the Co-op is winning lots of new customers on account of it.

Old-fashioned though it may sound, the Co-op Dividend scheme is a real money-saver, particularly on high-unit-value items such as wine. 'Co-op Dividend is the most generous supermarket loyalty card, paying twice as much on average as other food retailers' schemes,' declares the Co-op's Manifesto. 'Cardholders earn cash back on all their purchases – triple Dividend of 3p for every £1 spent on Co-op Brand goods ...'

The Co-op has an online-purchase website, with special offers as well as 'a selection' from the full list of 500 or so wines and spirits: **www.co-opdrinks2u.com.** You can also telephone co-opdrinks2u on freephone 0800 083 0501.

RED WINES   UNDER £5

ARGENTINA

9 **Co-op Old Vines Sangiovese 2003** £4.49
Ripe cherry whiff reminiscent of Chianti from this well
concentrated, rounded and pure-tasting briary-minty
red. Good value.

8 **Lo Tengo Malbec 2002** £4.99
Amusing hologram label of moving tango dancers
shouldn't put you off this soft, mocha-alluding, dark-
fruit red that will make a partner for salsa dishes.

AUSTRALIA

9 **Co-op Southeastern Australia Merlot 2002** £4.79
Remarkably poised black-cherry, juicy and vigorous red
with 14% alcohol but no sign of the jamminess that
spoils far too many budget Aussie wines. This really
stands out for its silky, edgy style.

FRANCE

9 **Co-op Vin de Pays d'Oc
Cabernet Sauvignon 2002** £3.89
Deliciously healthy and vigorous blackcurranty wine of
exceptional poise and intensity at such a modest price.

8 **Co-op Vin de Pays des Côtes Catalanes** £2.99
Lightweight, 11.5% alcohol, yet a gripping, briskly
fruity refresher with good intensity.

ITALY

9 **Co-op Puglia Primitivo-Sangiovese 2002** £4.49
Dark and satisfying, roasty-fruit rustic red that the
Co-op says has 'ripe aromas of spice and loganberry'.
Fair comment.

RED WINES   £5 PLUS

USA

🍷7 **The Boulders Reserve Shiraz 2002**   £5.49
One of a new range of screwcap wines from California
adopted by the Co-op, this is the pick of the reds, a big,
dark spicy one with robust flavours of blackberry and
(note) 14.5% alcohol.

S AFRICA

🍷8 **Co-op Cape Seal Bay Reserve Shiraz 2002** £6.99
Big smoothie has the ripeness under control to give a
lush, spicy poised effect. 'Try it with griddled ostrich
steak' recommends the back label.

SPAIN

🍷8 **Rioja Cuvée Nathalie 2002**   £6.99
Nathalie Estribeau is the French maker of this 100%
Tempranillo, which I think owes some its style to
Australian Shiraz! But this is a good, weighty young
blackberry red.

PINK WINES   UNDER £5

ARGENTINA

🍷10 **Argento Chardonnay 2003**   £4.99
I just cannot fault this consistently brilliant bargain from
top producer Catena. It has inviting yellow colour, a
theatrically elevated nose, and big apple-strudel-style,
nifty crisp finish. Cheap at the price.

🍷8 **Co-op Argentine Chardonnay-**
     Torrontes 2002   £3.79
This blend with ubiquitous Chardonnay works because
you get the peachy plushness of Torrontes combined
with a crisp apple keenness and citrus acidity from the
Chardonnay. A crowd-pleaser.

CHILE

♆8 Co-op Chilean Gewürztraminer 2003 £4.49
Lightweight, lychee-scented off-dry style to this spicy, exotic conversation piece to drink as an aperitif or with oriental food.

♆8 Chileno Sauvignon Blanc 2003 £4.99
Plenty of nettly zing and a respectable weight of grassy fruit in this well wrought dry wine.

FRANCE

♆9 Atlantique Sauvignon Blanc 2003 £4.99
Really brisk and enlivening grassy dry white with a fine lemony rim to the seaside flavour.

S AFRICA

**♆8 Sweet Surrender Pudding Wine 2003
half bottle** £4.99
Well contrived gold-coloured stickie has honey notes and is grapy rather than sweet. With artful balance of citrus acidity.

SPAIN

♆8 Torres Viña Sol 2003 £4.99
Cracking new vintage of this constant dry white from Spain's best winemaker, Miguel Torres. It's wholly un-Spanish, in an aromatic style reminiscent of the best kind of Alsace Pinot Blanc. As sunny and refreshing as it sounds. Screwcap.

Majestic

The Majestic empire continues to expand, with 120 'warehouses' throughout the country – an Inverness store opened in 2004 – averaging annual sales worth nearly £1 million per outlet.

It's a unique operation, selling wine by the case in any mix you like and any quantity from 12 bottles upwards. It's a very practical way to buy wine, and every branch has a car park, overcoming the disadvantage suffered by most high street retailers, that pedestrian customers can only take home as much wine as they can carry on and off the bus.

Majestic is a sort of supermarket chain of wine – they provide supermarket-style trolleys to accumulate your shopping in – but they don't sell anything else, barring a few beers and spirits.

And there is a formidable choice, from some of the best 'house' wines around the £3 mark to some very posh wines indeed. Every store has a huge range of champagnes, plus much wider choices from the classic French regions – Bordeaux, Burgundy and the Rhône – than any supermarket can aspire to. At the very top end, Majestic have lately opened a new Fine Wine Centre in St John's Wood, London, where classed growth clarets and a quite wonderful range of red and white burgundies are on offer at awesome prices. All the wines, incidentally, can be bought online at **www.majestic.co.uk** as well.

Majestic have opened a dozen new outlets in the last year. The shops are all over Britain except for the far south-east – Majestic have no wish to compete with the lure of the cross-Channel stores. At least not from England. So instead of setting up alongside the likes of Dave West's EastEnders warehouses, they have opened what are in effect three French Majestics – by the simple means of acquiring an existing business, Wine & Beer World. The stores are at Calais, Coquelles (west side of Calais) and Cherbourg.

By shopping at the French outlets you will save at least £1.50 on UK tags, so that, for example, the excellent Majestic Cuvée de Richard wines come down from £3.05 to £1.49. Champagnes are cut by as much as £10, and other pricier wines by impressive amounts. You can obtain a current list by ringing 01923 298297, or look up prices on the website and pre-order, so you simply turn up and collect the goodies.

And pricewise again, do bear in mind that Majestic are perpetually discounting their wines on a 'buy two save £1 (or whatever)' basis, so many of the prices quoted below may well be lower on the day.

RED WINES   UNDER £5

10 Cono Sur Pinot Noir 2003   **£4.69**
Close your eyes and you could be sniffing a good village burgundy – the earthy, strawberry aromas are a treat. Even the colour has the slightly weedy look of burgundy, but of course you get much more plump fruit than you would from the old country, especially at this price. A brilliant contrivance, and cheaper at Majestic than the universal £4.99-plus elsewhere.

9 Casillero del Diablo Carmenère 2003   **£4.99**
Another really cracking wine from this Concha y Toro range, this is near-black in colour, 14% alcohol and yet has a light touch, beguiling softness and a long lip-smacking finish. Bargain.

8 Casillero del Diablo Malbec 2003   **£4.99**
Soft, black-fruit and stimulatingly lively red.

CHILE

AUSTRALIA

8 **Griffin Vineyards Merlot 2003**   £4.99
Quite subtle in its balance of ripe fruit with clean acidity, this is a restrained plonk with easy appeal.

8 **Tiltili Cabernet Merlot Shiraz 2002**   £4.99
Near-opaque blend with tarry depths but plenty of fruit on top, and 14% alcohol.

FRANCE

10 **Cuvée de Richard Rouge 2003**   £3.05
Another excellent vintage of the Majestic house red vin de pays de l'Aude. It's brambly, balanced and bright with berry fruit – simply cannot be faulted.

9 **Cuvée des Amandiers Rouge 2003**   £3.49
Another consistent bargain, this is a vin de pays d'Oc with a dark fruit heart and a bit of tannic grip. Very good value.

8 **Grange du Midi Merlot 2003**   £3.99
Straight, ripe, sunny red with a hint of vanilla.

8 **Marc Ducournau Rouge 2003**   £4.49
Generous spicy glugger from Armagnac country has eager brightness of flavour.

ITALY

8 **Copertino, Masseria Monaci, 2000**   £4.99
Mature volcanic red with colour browning and sweet, tarry whiff, but plenty of gripping, dark fruit.

6 **Rosso di Sicilia, Cantine Settesoli, 2003**   £3.49
Generic Sicilian plonk made by the island's biggest producer, Settesoli, is everywhere and I've liked most of the bottles I've tasted from 2003, but this one seemed a bit too raisiny and even a little diluted. Probably just a bad bottle, but approach with caution.

S AFRICA

8 **Robertson Winery Merlot 2003** £4.99
Pleasant cherry-fruit slurper with an appreciable grip.

SPAIN

9 **Tempranillo Finca Tempranal 2002** £3.49
Classic blackcurrant-scented Tempranillo from the La Mancha wine lake, with a sweetly ripe strawberry heart. Bargain.

RED WINES   £5 PLUS

ARGENTINA

9 **Catena Cabernet Sauvignon 2001** £10.99
Still quite edgy with tannin, this perennial classic might just be a little more austere than previous vintages, but still a marvel of pure, slinky Cabernet.

AUSTRALIA

9 **Kangarilla Road Shiraz 2002** £9.99
A positively peppery and saucily plump smoothie with vigorous dark flavours – and a very fetching botanical label, it must be said.

CHILE

9 **Errazuriz Max Reserva Syrah 2000** £9.99
Blood red, this is a real prêt-à-porter wine, perfect to drink now with its artful balance of glossy mature fruit and lively bounciness.

8 **Winemaker's Lot Merlot,
Sol Vineyard, 2003** £7.99
Inky dark purple monster (14.5% alcohol) with plump, cushiony fruit and a roasty centre.

10 **Côtes du Rhône Villages Sablet,**
Domaine de Piaugier 2001 £6.49
Unusually dense colour for the appellation, and an exceptionally concentrated classic sunny-spicy fruit, too. Simply perfect CDR from a great vintage now benefiting from maturity. Snap this up while you can – subsequent vintages have been less auspicious.

9 **Beaujolais Lieu-Dit Tirefort,**
Cave de Bully 2003 £5.49
Fruit fairly bounces in this delicious basic Beaujolais from the first really good vintage the region has had in many years.

9 **Les Douze Fitou 2001** £5.99
Made by a team of 12 members of the famed Mont Tauch co-operative of Fitou, this is a broad, deep and spicy red without a hint of committee fudge. Rather extravagant intense fruit and expensive style. Terrific.

9 **Château de Gaudou Cuvée Renaissance,**
Cahors 2001 £8.99
Price has gone up £1 since the fabulous 2000 vintage, but I'm not begrudging it, because this is another very successful, opulent dark wine from what I believe to be the best estate in the Cahors appellation. Hints of leather, spice and creamy vanilla mingle with the concentrated black fruit, and will integrate all the better if you keep this potentially long-lived wine for a year or two. The 2002 vintage will follow, but I haven't tasted it.

9 **Marsannay Rouge, Domaine du Château**
du Marsannay 1999 £9.99
Wonderfully mature burgundy laden with cherry fruit, this is the sort of wine, in a smart bottle, that gives 'entry-level' burgundy a good name.

8 **Château Guiot, Costières de Nîmes 2003** £5.29
Gripping red with the slightly charred character that often marks out the excellent AC of Costières. Price seems to be creeping up, but a good perennial buy.

8 **Beaujolais Cuvée Vieilles Vignes,**
Cave de Bully 2003 £5.99
Relatively restrained and with a soft tannin grip, this has good raspberry fruit and a hint of white pepper.

8 **Bourgueil Les Cent Boisselées,**
Pierre-Jacques Druet 2002 £7.49
Sweet-natured Loire red already rounding out into a good balance of tannin and strawberry fruit.

8 **Château de Cray Bourgogne Rouge 2001** £7.99
Decent 'village' burgundy from the Chalonnais is earthy and mature.

8 **Premier Vin de Château de Pitray 1999** £8.49
Decent claret from an unfashionable corner of Bordeaux, the Côtes de Castillon, rather sadly labelled 'premier vin' – perhaps in vain protest at the fact that estates with smarter addresses can sell their 'deuxième vin' at twice this price even though it's no better. Anyway, a nice plump and rounded petit bourgeois wine for the money.

8 **Châteauneuf du Pape, Château de**
Beaucastel 2001 £35.00
Perhaps the most famous of all estates in Châteauneuf, this is a 'fine' wine already quite 'forward' in its development but not really for serious drinking until the end of the decade. It's terrifically good and cheap compared to Bordeaux counterparts.

ITALY

10 **Valpolicella Classico Superiore Ripasso,**
La Casetta di Ettore Righetti, 2000 £9.99
Plenty of heft in this big, juicy, raspberry-fruit reinforced
Valpolicella (Ripasso means there's a slug of super-
concentrated wine in it). Simply fabulous stuff.

8 **Bardolino Classico Tedeschi 2001** £5.49
Mature and untypically dense example of a once-
fashionable Veneto red has bright cherry fruit and good
dry edge.

8 **Promis Gaja 2001** £18.99
A Tuscan wine from Piedmont superstar Angelo Gaja,
this is cheap by his usual standards and great stuff, with
a sweet chilli-pepper nose and long Chianti-style
flavours.

NEW ZEALAND

9 **Oyster Bay Merlot 2002** £7.99
New Zealand Merlot is still rather a rarity, and this one
is rarely delicious – slinky, lush, cool and minty, with
that rush of pure, mineral fruit unique to the Kiwi
method. It's 14% alcohol and comes in a screwcap
bottle.

9 **Waimea Estate Pinot Noir 2002** £9.99
A new name to me, and a revealingly good Pinot with
darkness, density, 14% alcohol and the glossy, minty,
eucalyptus style of the Kiwi version of red burgundy.
Exciting stuff.

S AFRICA

8 **Goats du Roam in Villages 2002** £6.99
Winemaker and goat farmer Charles Back aims to make
Rhône-style wines in the Cape, and enjoys annoying the
French with names imitating those of their sacred
appellations. This very dark red has intensity and
spiciness, might be just a little stewed (14% alcohol) and
is good, hearty fun – a step up from standard bestseller
Goats du Roam.

SPAIN

9 **Mas Collet Celler de Capçanes 2001** £6.49
Cassis syrup smell to this very dark, oaked red is
followed up by a balanced fruit of elegant weight. This
is great stuff.

PINK WINES	UNDER £5

FRANCE

8 **Château La Gravette Rosé 2003** £4.49
Livid colour and a fresh, invigorating smell on this
gripping fresh pink from Minervois in the Languedoc.

7 **Cuvée des Amandiers Rosé 2003** £3.49
Smoked salmon colour to this mild-mannered vin de
pays d'Oc, with price the main attraction.

ITALY

8 **Pinot Grigio Rosé Adagio 2003** £4.99
Pink wine from a white grape? It's a sort of orange-coral
colour and actually tastes like Pinot Grigio – cunningly
appealing to concurrently fashionable PG and rosé
wines.

PINK WINES   UNDER £5

CHILE

9 **Santa Rita Cabernet Sauvignon Rosé 2003** **£5.85**
Attractive coral colour and lush strawberry fruit in this
vivid pink wine – full of life and charm.

FRANCE

8 **Château de Sours Rosé 2003** **£7.99**
Magenta-coloured, forcefully flavoured Bordeaux pink
is blackcurrant and satisfying, a proper wine rather
than a compromise.

WHITE WINES   UNDER £5

ARGENTINA

9 **Finca Las Moras Viognier 2003** **£4.99**
Seductive, just-dry wine with typical preserved-apricot
style of Viognier and long flavour.

AUSTRALIA

9 **Griffin Vineyards Chardonnay 2003** **£4.99**
Tasted among a lot of much more expensive Australian
wines, this bargain stood up very well indeed for
liveliness and interest.

9 **Griffin Vineyards Verdelho 2003** **£4.99**
Particularly likable, tropically perfumed, fleetingly
petrolly and mellow-flavoured off-dry white of
character.

8 **Coldridge Estate Chardonnay 2003** **£3.79**
A brightly fresh and unfaultable Aussie Chardy at an
unfaultable price.

CHILE

8 Casillero del Diablo
Sauvignon Blanc 2003 £4.69
Generous briny-grassy fruit in this mellow-finishing but fresh Sauvignon.

8 Casillero del Diablo Chardonnay 2003 £4.99
Cool but generous straight Chardonnay with notes of tropical fruits.

8 Cono Sur Viognier 2003 £4.99
Apple-pie whiff from this fruit salad of a wine with sweet notes and dry finish. Nicely rounded and 14% alcohol.

FRANCE

9 Cuvée de Richard Blanc 2003 £3.05
Brilliant house dry white from Toulouse area is craftily contrived from boring Colombard and Ugni Blanc to make a fresh, lively and crisp everyday plonk.

8 Cuvée des Amandiers Blanc 2003 £3.49
Decent, fresh seafood-matching vin de pays d'Oc, in which I fancied I detected a note of blanched almonds amid the fruit.

8 Marc Ducournau Vin de Pays
des Côtes de Gascogne 2003 £4.49
Particularly fresh, grassy-green-fruit dry white with more than expected substance, from an exceptional harvest.

GERMANY

10 Falkensteiner Riesling Freidrich Wilhelm
Gymnasium 2000 £4.99
Richly coloured, ripe and exotic racy moselle has the faintest waft of petrol and inner notes of honey, altogether making for a fantastic bargain.

9 Garganega Pinot Grigio delle Venezie Antica Corte 2003 £4.39

I very much liked this sunny and zestful PG, even though it doesn't quite fit the expected mould – just a really likeable bargain.

8 Bianco di Sicilia Cantine Settesoli 2003 £3.49

Soft and easy herbaceous dry white of good quality for the price.

8 Chardonnay di Sicilia Cantine Settesoli 2003 £4.99

There is gold colour and fruit to match in this lipsmacking ripe slurper.

8 Robertson Winery Chenin Blanc 2003 £3.99

Very decent florally scented off-dry white with mellow fruit.

8 Montgomery Creek Chardonnay 2003 £3.99

Unusally good Californian cheapie has straight appley fruit with hints of richness.

ITALY

S AFRICA

USA

WHITE WINES **£5 PLUS**

9 Catena Barrel Fermented Chardonnay 2002 £10.99

Perennial classic has passed the £10 mark for the first time, but it's still a great buy, extravagantly rich and lingering, with perfect acidity.

ARGENTINA

AUSTRALIA

8 **Cape Mentelle Semillon Sauvignon 2002** £10.99
Famous wine with flavours as diverse as peach and asparagus, and the sort of weight and dimension you expect for this kind of money.

CHILE

8 **Montes Reserve Sauvignon Blanc 2003** £5.79
Gooseberry-fool flavours in this soft-finishing but refreshing wine with a lot of ripeness and 14% alcohol.

8 **Montes Alpha Chardonnay 2002** £9.99
A big yellow rich wine with 14.5% alcohol and enough luxurious weight to merit the price.

ENGLAND

8 **Curious Grape Empire Zest 2001** £5.49
The name leaves me perplexed, but the wine is excellent, apple-crisp and lively, interest and just 11% alcohol.

FRANCE

10 **Rully 1er Cru Vieilles Vignes**
Vincent Girardin, 2002 £11.99
Another simply fabulous burgundy (Chalonnais region) with plush fruit and stone-pure minerality – really elegant wine wearing its ripeness (14% alcohol) lightly.

9 **St-Véran Orchys 2002** £8.99
Among a large number of good Mâconnais whites tasted, this one stood out: a well coloured Chardonnay with powerful pineapple and peach aroma and lavish but pebbly-fresh creamy fruit. Sinfully good burgundy.

9 **Alsace Riesling Grand Cru Eichberg**
Zinck 2002 £9.99
Rare Alsace classic has lush fruit lurking one layer under the crisp entry to the flavour of this complex, wildly aromatic dry wine.

**St-Aubin Blanc 1er Cru Gérard Thomas
2002** £11.49

Classic burgundy in which the lemony acidity pierces the lush fruit to give a thrilling flavour balance.

 **Alsace Gewürztraminer Grand Cru
Sonnenglanz Bott-Geyl 2001** £17.99

All credit to Majestic for stocking this esoteric wine, which by the way is utterly wonderful – yellow-gold, clouds of lychee perfume, cornucopia of ripe spicy fruit.

 **Menetou-Salon Domaine Henry Pellé
2003** £8.49

Posh Sauvignon Blanc from a fashionable appellation is nettly, green-tinged and memorably vivid.

 **Bourgogne Blanc Cuvé St Vincent
Vincent Girardin 2002** £8.99

This grand Chardonnay culminates in a superb citrus acidity that really wakes the tastebuds.

**Sancerre Clos des Bouffants
Domaine Roger Neveu 2003** £9.49

Majestic have more than 20 different Sancerres, including reds and rosés, and this is among the more affordable. Big ripe Sauvignon with long-reaching gooseberry fruit.

**Urziger Würzgarten Riesling Auslese
Christoffel-Berres 1997** £6.99

Crisp and spritzy apple-strudel Moselle with a thrilling note of honeysuckle – delicious refresher with a streak of insinuating sweetness.

FRANCE

GERMANY

ITALY

8 **Verdicchio dei Castelli di Jesi**
Coste del Molino 2003 £5.49
Lots of lively vegetal fruit in this substantial dry wine, fresh and distinctive.

8 **Bianco di Custoza Cavalchina 2003** £5.59
Better than most Soave, of which this wine is a sort of declassified version, with zest and crispness.

8 **Gavi di Gavi Raccolto Tardivo**
Villa Lanata 2003 £7.99
Richly ripe 'late harvest' dry white with long lively flavours.

NEW ZEALAND

9 **Oyster Bay Sauvignon Blanc 2003** £6.99
Famed dry white is typically zesty, with a distinctive whiff of grapefruit and concentrated flavours including asparagus, gooseberry and a hint of kiwi fruit! Screwcap.

9 **Waimea Estate Sauvignon Blanc 2003** £8.99
Grassy-gooseberry, super-zesty wine with massive, lingering fruit and a nifty nettly finish.

S AFRICA

8 **The Maverick Chenin Blanc 2003** £6.99
Oaky, sweetly ripe monster (14.5% alcohol) that I am convinced would make an ideal partner with rare roast beef and horseradish!

SPAIN

10 **Hidalgo La Gitana Manzanilla Sherry** £6.49
The tangiest, tastiest pale bone-dry sherry of them all, from seaside bodega at Sanlucar de Barrameda, is an inimitably great aperitif to drink fresh and chilled.

8 **Rioja Blanco Muga 2003** £6.99
Fresh and tangy modern-style white Rioja also has creamy depths from barrel-fermentation.

— Marks & Spencer —

No doubt M&S would rather have been less in the news than it has been of late. But the old firm deserves a lot of positive attention for its wines, which are just getting better and better, and maintaining their outstanding value for money.

All the wines are 'unique and exclusive', in M&S's own words. That is, they are all own-labels, in keeping with the company's policy of selling only one 'brand' in its stores, namely the Marks & Spencer brand.

The producers of the basic wines include a lot of well-known giants of the business – Domaines Virginie in France, Girelli in Italy, Southcorp in Australia and so on – but there are many individual estates with M&S listings, too, and these are frequently very well sought out. As with all the supermarket chains, the more esoteric wines will only be available from the largest stores.

There is a constantly rolling programme of promotional discounts on wines in all the stores, with prices regularly reduced by 20 per cent, so do always check out the offers when popping in for a sandwich or new woolly.

Chances are that in larger branches there will be a specially trained Wine Advisor to help you with your choice, which seems a good idea, giving M&S a useful edge over other supermarkets. And given that the Marks's wine range is so much its own, there seems every likelihood that these advisers will know what they're talking about.

/RED WINES   UNDER £5

AUSTRALIA

9   Weandre Stream Shiraz 2002   £4.99
Friendly briary glugger with ideal fruit-dryness balance;
in spite of 14% alcohol it has an almost French restraint.

8   Burra Brook Shiraz 2003   £4.99
Such a strong liquorice taste in the centre of this, but
there's cushiony fruit on top.

ITALY

9   Vino da Tavola Rosso   £3.29
Ribena-coloured, sunny strawberry-fruit plonk with lots
of life, this is brisk, clean and healthy, and impressively
cheap.

8   Negroamaro del Salento 2003   £3.99
Dark and coaly deep-south red with satisfying weight
and clean finish.

SPAIN

8   Palacio del Marques Bobal Cabernet 2003 £3.99
Interesting dry red with blackcurrant contribution from
Cabernet but lots of nice bouncy soft flavour,
presumably from mysterious Bobal grape, and good dry
finish.

RED WINES   £5 PLUS

ARGENTINA

8   Tupungato Cabernet Malbec 2003   £5.99
Leather and liquorice count among the evocations from
this dusky 14% alcohol red, which would go well with
chilli dishes – a fun wine, well worth a try.

8   Canale Estate Reserve Merlot 2002   £9.99
Spicy-leathery top flavour on this black-cherry monster
with 14% alcohol. Lots of oak evident, though not
masking the generous fruit. Will develop for years.

9 **Wickham Estate Shiraz 1999** £13.99

Colour's going chocolate in this bravura mature red, affording a rare chance to see what can happen to great Aussie wine if you give it time. Lovely ripe and spicy, strong (14.5% alcohol) red of grand character.

8 **Kalleske Estate Barossa Valley Organic Shiraz 2002** £8.99

Deceptively light colour but a big cassis red of immense ripeness (14.5% alcohol) and grip.

8 **Domaine des Fontsèque Corbières 2001** £9.99

Ten quid for a Corbières! But this is a grand wine, heavy with garrigue-influenced rich flavours and still with a young, liquorice centre. Gripping stuff made by ex-rugby star Gerard Bertrand.

8 **Bandol Domaine Bunan 2000** £12.99

Bold black-fruit Provençal red has massive, luxury flavours, and will surely continue to develop for many years, but lovely now. This is the wine sipped by hedonistic millionaires along the Côte d'Azur, and to drink it is to understand a little of why the rich really do have more fun.

9 **Evangelo Single Estate 2003** £9.99

Big young wine with lurid maroon colour and still with tannic tension, but it's absolutely gorgeous, brimming with rich, velvet fruit, and suggesting strongly that Greece is capable of Olympian heights in the wine game.

7 **Dipnon Merlot 2003** £5.99

Strong, tannic red that might just stand up to a moussaka, with the mouth-puckering finish a suitable counterpoint to the olive oil.

10 **Wolvenbosch Family Vineyards Shiraz 2002** £6.99

It's like sniffing a bubbling vat of blackberry jam, then it gets even better – dark, wicked, glossy red with a black heart and long, consistent plummy-spicy fruit. Great wine that does not betray its strength (15% alcohol), so beware.

S AFRICA

9 **Houdamond Pinotage 2000** £6.99

Silky smoothie still has a grip of tannin in spite of relative maturity and skeins of flavour – true Pinotage of real quality at a good price.

PINK WINES	UNDER £5

AUSTRALIA

8 **Burra Brook Rosé 2003** £4.99

Rich coral colour and a gripping red berry fruit that suggests this is one to drink with food – and in moderation as it has 14.5% alcohol.

CHILE

8 **Casa Leona Rosé 2003** £4.99

Magenta colour, good, gripping blackcurrant fruit and plenty of character.

9 **Fino Sherry** £4.99

Very tangy and fresh fino by Williams and Humbert, this is almost salty on the nose. Really lively bone-dry sherry at a giveaway price.

9 **Manzanilla Sherry** £4.99

Classic bone-dry style with slaking flavour and the tang of briny freshness appropriate to sherry made by the seaside at Sanlucar de Barrameda.

SPAIN

SPAIN

7 Las Falleras Rosé 2003 £2.99

Pale petal colour, confectionery smell, soft strawberry fruit.

PINK WINES	£5 PLUS

FRANCE

8 Domaine Verlaque Provence Rosé 2003 £5.99

Colour put me in mind of rosewater, but fruit is a lot more intense than that – flinty, flowery and with a middle flavour of cassis. Jolly nice.

WHITE WINES	UNDER £5

ARGENTINA

9 Argentine Pinot Grigio 2003 £4.99

This has an unrevealing smell, and the first thing you sense about the flavour is the lemony rim of acidity. Then comes a positive, charmingly ripe middle fruit. And you're away. Better than just about anything Italian at this price.

AUSTRIA

8 Grüner Veltliner Niederösterreich 2003 £4.99

Soft, eggy aromatic dry white with a nice zesty prickle in the flavour – thought-provoking.

FRANCE

9 Domaine Mandeville Viognier 2003 £3.99

Dynamic vin de pays d'Oc with intriguing balance of marrowy richness and zest that mark out well made Viognier. Super quality at this price. Screwcap.

9 Touraine Sauvignon Blanc 2003 £4.99

Amazingly bright, straightforward wine with the zip if not the depth of much pricier rivals. I even liked the endearing déjeuner-sur-l'herbe-themed label. Screwcap.

FRANCE

8 **Dry Muscat 2003** £4.99
It really is dry, but you also get the elusive grapy-ambrosial aftertaste of the exotic fruit.

HUNGARY

9 **Hungarian Pinot Grigio 2003** £3.99
This is a cracker – healthy straw colour, lively, smoky, spicy nose and plenty of corresponding fruit. Soft sort of finish, otherwise I would give it 10, but it will please most drinkers very much.

9 **Quadro Sei Gavi 2003** £4.99
Nice inviting melon nose and a big mouthful of matching fruit – stacks of flavour and interest in this dry, invigorating Piedmont white.

ITALY

9 **Racina Ianca Grillo Sicilia 2003** £4.99
Lots of flavour here, including pineapple, asparagus and peach. It's ripe and fresh, and in a sea of boring Italian whites, well worth trawling for.

8 **Villa Masera Organic 2003** £4.49
Grassy dry white from the grape that goes into Soave, and refreshingly bright.

SPAIN

9 **Palacio del Marques Macabeo**
Chardonnay 2003 £3.99
A rather cerebral dry white for the money, with good colour, herbaceous aroma and layered vegetal-appley flavours.

8 **Torresoto Unwooded White Rioja 2003** £4.99
Not the oxidised style of the old days but a fresh and crisp dry white in which the richness of the constituent Viura grape is agreeably invasive.

WHITE WINES	£5 PLUS

ARGENTINA

♆9 Tupungato Chardonnay 2002 £5.99

Nice gold colour, and an almost burgundian balance to the fruit and oak. Elegant, reassuring wine.

AUSTRALIA

♆8 Coonawarra Vineyards Riesling 2003 £5.49

Flinty but generously full flavours in this balanced textbook Aussie dry Riesling.

♆8 Banwell Farm Riesling 2003 £7.99

Convincing case for spending a bit more to get a bit more, this has superb floral perfume and forceful limey minerality that make for an exciting glassful.

AUSTRIA

♆8 Chardonnay Trockenbeerenauslese 2002 £15

Ambrosial 'dessert' wine with gold colour, honeyed flavours and a well wrought clean finish. Expensive, and from a grape variety not normally associated with this sort of thing, but comparable with Sauternes for quality and value.

CHILE

♆8 Sierra los Andes Chardonnay 2003 £5.99

Sweetly oaked formulaic Chardy is made above-average by its heightened minerality.

FRANCE

♆9 Vouvray Domaine de la Pouvraie 2003 £5.50

This is dry, but nevertheless has a mound of lush floral flavours and nectareous undertones – lovely summer white of great charm.

♆8 Cave de Turckheim Alsace Riesling 2003 £5.99

Nice pointy flavour in this tangy, stimulating, dry aromatic wine at a keen price.

9 **Mineralstein Riesling Matthias Gaul 2003** £6.99

Lovely generic wine with amazingly full fruit, lush apple-pie depths and, I promise, a mineral freshness.

9 **Ernst Loosen Zeltinger Himmelreich Riesling 2003** £9.99

Piquant apple nose and gorgeous rich-but-racy Riesling fruit in this vaulting Moselle, lovely now and capable of developing, and 8.5% alcohol.

8 **Darting Estate Riesling Dürkheimer Michelsberg 2003** £5.99

Modern limey-style Rhine wine with lots of vigorous appley fruit and dry finish.

8 **Rüdesheim Estate Bernhard Breuer Riesling 2002** £8.99

Crisp apple style revealing a deliciously long, unwinding racy Riesling fruit in the depths. This is a treat.

7 **Dipnon Roditis Riesling 2003** £5.99

Gooseberry character to this fresh and vigorous curiosity from the shores of the Gulf of Corinth.

7 **Zefiros Assyrtiko Sauvignon Blanc 2003** £9.99

A Hellenic quest for the grail that is good Sauvignon, this has a volcanic nuance, plenty of vivid grassy fruit and proverbial crispness.

8 **Basilicata Dry Muscat 2003** £5.99

Sweet, musky nose of the Muscat grape but a decidedly dry flavour with marmalade suggestions.

GERMANY

GREECE

ITALY

8 **Friuli Pinot Grigio 2003** £5.99

Sweetly seductive nose and big, properly concentrated fruit on a well-above-average PG.

10 **Kaituna Hills Reserve Sauvignon Blanc 2003** £7.99

Amazing asparagus nose and a blast of classic green Kiwi Sauvignon as good as any I've tasted all year. Utterly consistent flavour and lipsmacking finish. Simply perfect and very good price.

8 **Kaituna Hills Chardonnay 2003** £5.99

Grand sleek shock-of-appley-fruit Chardy with creamy depths.

8 **Kaituna Hills Riesling 2003** £5.99

Lemony-spiky and very fresh limey dry white. Screwcap.

8 **Torresoto Barrel Fermented White Rioja 2002** £6.99

Throwback yellow colour, oxidised nose and creamy-vanilla fruit in this reactionary Rioja. If you like the style, you'll love this wine.

8 **Terra Douro Albariño 2003** £8.99

Brisk grassy fruit, signature of the fashionable Albariño grape, is to the fore in this almost aggressively green but very delicious cult wine.

—Morrisons & Safeway—

Morrisons got the go-ahead from its own shareholders, and those of Safeway, to take over its larger rival in March 2004 for the piffling sum of £3 billion.

Safeway stores have already begun to disappear, or rebrand, as the deal takes effect. Early reports indicated that 118 of the larger supermarkets will turn into Morrisons, 171 mid-size stores will be reborn as Morrisons Choice, and the smallest stores will keep the Safeway name for the moment; 53 stores are being sold off.

Morrisons reckons to have a range of 500 different wines, of which more than 100 are priced at under £3. Sales of wine increased by 21 per cent in the last year alone. Although the chain makes its name on cheap wines, dominated by the New World, the stores are clearly a place of pilgrimage for the more serious-minded wine-bargain hunter, because the fastest-growing regional wines – all up by at least 30 per cent last year – have been red burgundies, Beaujolais, Alsace and Champagne.

Because the chain is in a state of flux, integrating its wine range with that of Safeway, there has been no wine tasting for the likes of me this year, and so I have nothing to report on this front, for which many apologies. No doubt this will be fully remedied in the next edition of this guide.

Sainsbury's

There are some spectacularly good red wines from Australia and Chile in Sainsbury's 'mid-price' range – £6 to £9 – at the moment, and these are among several features that continue to make this supermarket special as a place to buy wine.

Other highlights are a hugely expanded range of red wines from Spain, including more than a dozen Riojas, and a very large choice of white wines from Germany. It's true that the numbers are substantially made up of well-known universal brands, but here and there are superb bargains such as Campaneo Old Vines Garnacha from the edge of Rioja country and Dr L Riesling from the Mosel. Both these wines happen to be priced at £5.99, and it's at this level that Sainsbury's really does offer a good choice.

RED WINES   UNDER £5

CHILE

8 **Sainsbury's Chilean Merlot** £2.99
Slightly hard-edged, non-vintage plonk, but with a sunny
and ripe core fruit that really appeals. You get a good
balanced glug for your money.

8 **Sainsbury's Chilean Cabernet Sauvignon** £2.99
Gritty stuff, more French in style than Latin, with a
stalky element in the fruit, but a really good crisp
Cabernet and very cheap.

FRANCE

8 **Vin de Pays des Côtes Catalanes** £2.99
Non-vintage, hearty red from deep south is rustic and
thoroughly likable at this price.

8 **Le Petit Sommelier Soft Fruity Red 2002** £3.99
Pale, but not wan, bright and brisk vin de pay d'Oc that
turns out rather better than the curious branding might
lead you to believe.

8 **Réserve St Marc Grenache Malbec 2003** £4.49
Breezy lightweight vin de pays d'Oc that can be served
cool.

7 **La Chasse du Pape Syrah 2003** £4.99
Spicy highlights in this otherwise softly textured vin de
pays d'Oc with a dry edge.

PORTUGAL

9 **Sainsbury's Premium Portuguese Red 2001** £3.99
Self-effacingly presented but jolly good little regional
wine with flavour elements including cloves and Victoria
plums (skins on). A delicious bargain.

10 St Hallett Faith Cabernet Sauvignon 2001   £6.99
This is simply perfect. Clarety whiff, beautiful poised minty-cedary fruit, with a thrilling ripe core to the flavour. The complete Barossa Valley all-rounder at an unimpeachable price.

10 St Hallett Old Block Shiraz 2000   £14.99
Apotheosis. Winemaking like this puts Australia on a par with any other nation. It's pricy, but this Barossa is a match for its French counterpart, Côte Rôtie, and with this sort of maturity (2000 vintage is ancient history Down Under) would undercut it in price by half. Simply fabulous wine, available only from the 50 biggest stores.

9 Wirra Wirra Sexton's Acre Shiraz 2002   £6.99
Gripping, spicy, dry-but-rich Barossa red with well contrived finish, this is a profoundly satisfying wine of 14.5% alcohol. Screwcap, and a nice jampot-style label.

9 St Hallett Faith Shiraz 2002   £7.99
Love the dark heart to the flavour of this sumptuous peppery wine – the flavour is consistent and captivating.

9 Wirra Wirra Church Block
Cabernet Sauvignon Shiraz Merlot 2002   £9.99
Near-black colour and with a superb sun-ripened blackberry nose. This is tangy with liveliness and immensely concentrated with a dark liquorice heart, yet of easy weight, although 14.5% alcohol. Screwcap.

8 Sainsbury's Classic Selection
Western Australia Cabernet Merlot 2003   £6.99
Bumper blend with roasted but not overcooked ripe fruit, 14.5% alcohol and a light touch.

AUSTRALIA

8 **Skuttlebutt Cabernet Sauvignon-Shiraz-Merlot 2002** £6.99

Nice balance of fruit and acidity in this curiously named blend with a friendly balance of density and weightlessness. Screwcap.

CHILE

9 **Tabali Cabernet Sauvignon Reserva 2002** £6.99

Lovely minty Cabernet with pure cassis style and a great edge of acidity with 14% alcohol. The purity of the fruit jumps out at you.

9 **Doña Dominga Carmenère Reserve 2002** £7.99

It's the colour and almost the density of blood, with raspberry, maybe even loganberry, nose and huge, pulpy dense fruit – a really plausible soft and squishy monster red.

8 **Tabali Syrah Reserva 2002** £6.99

Approachable, spicy softie with grip and depth of fruit. Dense, and 14% alcohol, but awfully easy to drink.

8 **Don Reca Limited Release Merlot 2002** £8.99

Peppery heavyweight (14.5% alcohol) with lots of heart and convincing balance between ripeness and briskness.

7 **Santa Rita 120 Carmenère 2003** £5.99

Dense, deep maroon colour, syrupy nose, but a distinctly dry-finishing brambly fruit. I suspect this big wine (14% alcohol) is better than gathered on first taste.

FRANCE

8 **Côtes du Rhône Domaine des Coccinelles
2002** **£5.99**
Ladybird label will attract buyers to this nice, spicy, dark
red with sunny fruit – no doubt it will be known as
beetle juice.

ITALY

8 **Brolio Chianti Classico Barone Ricasoli
2002** **£10.99**
Very dense maroon colour to this dark-hearted young
red with classic minty Chianti character. Very nice wine
from the estate where Chianti originates – thus,
presumably, the premium price.

7 **Barbera d'Alba Vigna Fontanelle Ascheri
2001** **£8.49**
Densely coloured, bramble-fruit, dry-finishing Pied-
montese red is quite austere but has character. Especially
well suited to pasta.

PORTUGAL

9 **Quinta do Crasto Touriga Nacional 2001 £14.99**
Top-flight Douro red of outstanding quality is big, dark
and beautifully pitched. Lovely now and will be for years
to come.

8 **Quinta do Crasto Reserva Old Vines
2001** **£11.99**
Dense, porty colour and an almost spiritous nose, but
this Douro red is definitely table wine – though 14.5%
alcohol – and is extravagantly delicious, with minty
damson fruit. Good now, and will improve.

7 **Sainsbury's Classic Selection Douro 2001 £6.99**
Lots of dark tannin on the edge of this port-country
table wine. Like the best kind of port, I'd keep it a few
years in the likelihood it will turn out very well.

S AFRICA

8   **Kumala Organic Pinotage Shiraz 2003**   £5.99
Interesting tarry-spicy style to the dark, plump fruit in this handsome Cape big brand. It has guts and long likable flavours.

SPAIN

9   **Campaneo Old Vines Garnacha,**
       Campo de Borja, 2003   £5.99
Beguiling blackberry fruit in this soft-centred, firm-edged monster (14% alcohol) that will be excellent with winter stews.

8   **Agramont Seleccion Navarra 2002**   £5.99
Challenging dry edge to the taste of this strawberry-scented heavyweight (14% alcohol) and long dark flavours. Good, strong wine from Rioja's humbler neighbour.

PINK WINES   **UNDER £5**

FRANCE

8   **Big Frank's Deep Pink 2003**   £3.99
Pale magenta colour, but this vin de pays d'Oc has a red-wine style as much as a pink one, and is none the worse for that.

8   **Lurton Cabernet Rosé 2003**   £3.99
Pale smoked salmon colour and a good whack of summer soft fruit finished with a gentle acidity – an easy, affordable, crowd-pleaser from the Loire.

7   **Rosé Domaine de Pellehaut 2003**   £4.99
Shocking pink Gascony vin de pays has taut and gripping fruit.

7 Enclave des Papes Côtes du Rhône Rosé 2003 £4.99

FRANCE

Confected-looking colour, simple direct strawberry fruit with a lightness of weight that belies the 14% alcohol.

8 Agramont Garnacha Rosado 2003 £3.99

SPAIN

Luminous colour, brisk and crisp Navarra pink with bright fruit – fresh, lively, likable.

PINK WINES   £5 PLUS

10 Torres San Medin Cabernet Sauvignon Rosé 2003 £5.49

CHILE

Magenta colour, nose of leafy Cabernet and, as per the claim on the back label, 'plums and cherries over a background of grapefruit' in the flavour. This is my pick of the pinks this year because it's real rosé, not a compromise, with eager flavour.

9 Domaine de Sours Rosé 2003 £5.49

FRANCE

Colour not far short of a pale red, this is wine-drinker's rosé from Bordeaux, not just something for those who can't decide between red and white. It's ripe and alive with soft fruit, leaving a good dry aftertaste and a strawberry memory.

7 Sainsbury's Australian Riesling 2003 £4.99

AUSTRALIA

Limey-tropical, substantial, budget dry wine with character. Screwcap.

FRANCE

9 **Sainsbury's Classic Selection Muscadet
Sèvre et Maine 2003** £4.99

There's a fair old twang of briny acidity in this, as well
as an enticing whiff of sweetness in the fruit. A big-
flavoured, bone-dry Muscadet of character.

8 **Castel Chardonnay Viognier Cuvée Réserve
2003** £4.99

Ripe, vegetal, dry vin de pays d'Oc has a good dollop of
the apricot richness that identifies the Viognier grape – a
good branded wine by the giant company that owns
Nicolas in France and Oddbins over here.

8 **La Baume Sauvignon Blanc 2003** £4.99

Good crisp 'attack' – first flavour sensation – in this
nettly and generous vin de pays d'Oc brand.

7 **Le Petit Sommelier Fruity White 2003** £3.99

Crisp, fresh vin de pays d'Oc lives up to the claim that
it's fruity.

GERMANY

10 **Villa Wolf Pinot Gris 2002** £4.99

I picked the 2001 vintage of this fabulous aromatic
Rhine wine as the best bargain of them all in last year's
edition of this guide. And what do Sainsbury's do? They
reduce the price from £5.99 to £4.99. OK, the shock of
the new has worn off, but this new vintage is another
great, characterful and seriously underpriced wine, and I
urge all to try it.

ITALY

9 **Sainsbury's Pinot Grigio delle Venezie 2003** £4.79

Now that Pinot Grigio has become so fashionable, it seems harder than ever to find a decent bottle under a fiver. But here's one with plenty of colour, a really attractive spicy aroma and corresponding fruit interest – lively and characterful.

S AFRICA

9 **Kumala Organic Colombard Chardonnay 2003** £4.99

Big Cape brand impresses with its rich colour and exuberant peachy-melony fruit. Scores high for freshness, too. It's always a relief to taste a big-name wine that is both good and good value.

WHITE WINES   £5 PLUS

8 **Leasingham Magnus Riesling 2003** £6.99

Exotic nose with a clear suggestion of petrol and lashings of limey, pineappley fruit – a delicious, ripe food wine.

AUSTRALIA

8 **Nepenthe Tryst Sauvignon Blanc Semillon 2003** £6.99

Nettly Sauvignon dominates the flavour but there's a relishable tropical touch from the Semillon contribution. Screwcap.

8 **Sainsbury's Classic Selection Western Australia Sauvignon Blanc Semillon 2003** £6.99

Cabbagey nose, asparagus fruit, grapefruit finish. Great wine, honestly, though rather let down by its downbeat label. Screwcap.

9   **Cono Sur Vision Gewürztraminer 2003**   £7.99
Tropical-style Gewürz with alluring lychee and peach perfume, exotic fruit and nifty acidity to make it purifying as well as complex. Long and fresh with a seductive note of residual sweetness.

9   **Santa Rita Medalla Real Sauvignon Blanc 2003**   £7.99
Positively enthralling gooseberry-asparagus nose on this hugely flavoursome cat's pee Sauvignon – very good stuff in its own, butch (14% alcohol) style.

8   **Cono Sur Vision Riesling 2002**   £7.99
Limey and pebbly, fresh bumper dry white with citrus rim to the flavour. Straight, pure New World Riesling but by no means one-dimensional. Screwcap.

7   **Gran Araucano Sauvignon Blanc 2002**   £8.99
Emphatic ripe fruit in this characterful wine, with vigour and length of flavour.

FRANCE

8   **Michel Laroche Chardonnay 2003**   £5.99
Plenty of woof in this assertive mineral vin de pays d'Oc, notable for its long, apple-crisp flavours.

GERMANY

🍷10 Dr L Riesling 2003 £5.99

Gorgeous ripe autumnal flavours in this poised toffee-apple moselle from Ernie Loosen, one of Germany's stellar winemakers. It is, I suppose, 'dry' but has long, lush flavours of many fruits. Outstanding wine with just 8.5% alcohol and a screwcap.

🍷9 Bert Simon Serrig Würtzberg Riesling
Kabinett 2001 £5.99

Superb, crisp-but-lush, appley-but-gently-honeyed, racy moselle with just 8% alcohol and 100% pure classic Riesling flavour. Great bargain.

🍷7 Querbach Hallgartener Halbtrocken
Riesling 2002 £8.49

Floral aroma and corresponding blossomy fruit in this 'half dry' Rhine wine – jolly good but less of a bargain than some other German wines at Sainsbury's.

Somerfield

Among the supermarket giants, Somerfield is the Cinderella. But the chain claims to be 'the UK's biggest high street food retailer' on the basis that nine out of every ten of its 690 stores are in town centre and suburban locations.

Somerfield's wine range, like the square-footage of its outlets, is significantly smaller than those of its Ugly Sisters, but there are plenty of good buys, especially among the own-label lines. This year, new own-labels that I have found particularly impressive include the Australian 'First Flight' range of 'entry-price' bargains, starting at the un-Australian price point of £2.99. And the Argentinian wines remain very impressive.

I have given 10 out of 10 scores to three wines unique to Somerfield: their brilliant German Dry Riesling, a spectacular sweet Australian Riesling, and a Californian Merlot that costs £4.99 and tastes like a £10 claret. And there are very many more outstanding wines in this line-up besides.

Somerfield has a perpetual programme of wine discounts, reducing prices by large margins. Interestingly, it is often the own-label wines that are promoted in this way – which makes a refreshing change from the usual boring big brands elsewhere. But note that Somerfield is currently in the process of establishing a customer loyalty scheme and has introduced a Saver Card, which you will need if you wish to qualify even for the standard price discounts. By completing a short application form, you will qualify for additional savings and offers related to your buying habits.

10 High Altitude Malbec Shiraz 2003   £4.99

Perfectly balanced, darkly rich and pure-tasting meaty red that screams quality. Argentine Malbecs can be a bit tough in this price range, but this one is positively insinuating, and the element of spicy Shiraz does a lot for it. Stonkingly good stuff. The brand is so-called because the vineyards are at 1,000 metres above sea level in the Andes foothills of Mendoza province.

9 Somerfield Argentine Sangiovese 2003   £3.99

Another good vintage of this cherry-scented, juicy and firmly finishing Italian-style middleweight from the Zuccardi family.

9 Trivento Reserve Syrah 2001   £4.99

Ritzy aroma and smoothed-out 'reserva' style to this bargain. It seems a luxury wine for the money, and the lively fruit has by no means been oaked out of it.

8 Argento Malbec 2003   £4.99

Perennial quality red with a hint of leather but nevertheless with a soft, obliging fruit. A wine it pays to decant.

8 High Altitude Cabernet Tempranillo 2002   £4.99

Wild-fruit, remarkably concentrated red with chocolatey, black-cherry mid-flavours. A bit syrupy but fun.

8 Santa Julia Oak Aged Tempranillo 2003   £4.99

Purple-bright colour to this pure-fruit blackcurrant red, marked by a juicy style and brisk finish.

ARGENTINA

8 **Terra Organica Bonarda Sangiovese 2003** **£4.99**
Successful blend in which the Bonarda grape plumps up
the cherry-nutty style of the Sangiovese into a pleasing
soft red. Zuccardi again.

9 **Somerfield First Flight Red 2003** **£2.99**
Dark wine with lots of alcohol (14%) but none of the
anticipated cooked overripeness in a wine this cheap.
Hefty but not clumping, up-front but not outrageous, it's
a successful 'entry-price' red for everyday glugging.

8 **Somerfield First Flight Cabernet Sauvignon
2002** **£3.99**
Cool and minty style belies high alcohol (14%) and
makes for a summery, juicy and bright red with
recognisably blackcurrant character.

8 **Somerfield First Flight Reserve Shiraz
2002** **£4.99**
Again, 14% alcohol, but this is a rather restrained style,
poised blackberry fruit with a white pepper note. Not
very 'Australian' and definitely likable.

7 **Somerfield First Flight Shiraz Cabernet
2002** **£3.99**
Slightly sweet, with high alcohol (14%), but smooth and
easy. Screwcap.

9 **Somerfield Chilean Merlot 2003** **£4.03**
Ripe straight Merlot at a great price – scores high as an
everyday red. Shame about the plastic cork.

FRANCE

8 **Goûts et Couleurs Syrah Mourvèdre 2002** **£4.49**
In spite of the silly brand name, a good firm vin de pays
d'Oc with uplifted cherry nose and pleasing ripe flavour.

8 **Vacqueyras Vignerons Beaumes de Venise
2002** **£4.99**
Low price for a wine from the prestigious Rhône village
of Vacqueyras. And it's pretty good, with plenty of dark
peppery fruit.

MEXICO

8 **LA Cetto Petite Sirah 2001** **£4.99**
Very dark wine from Baja California has raspberry-
ripple nose, a grip of tannin, lots of friendly fruit and just
a hint of raisiny overripeness, but a properly authentic
wine to drink with chilli and tacos.

PORTUGAL

9 **Pedras do Monte 2002** **£4.49**
Typically dark and spicy Portuguese red with appealing
eucalyptus character that makes such a good match for
exotic Iberian food.

USA

10 **Leaping Horse Merlot 2001** **£4.99**
The only thing I don't love about this wine is the lurid
purple plastic cork. Otherwise perfect, it has a light
colour (by California standards) and elegant, leafy
aroma followed up by poised, minty-morello Merlot
fruit of striking balance and purity. An unexpected
winner.

RED WINES   £5 PLUS

AUSTRALIA

9 **Palandri Estate Merlot 2001**   £6.99
Lovely, beckoning black-cherry nose and velvet, focused juicy fruit like an unusually endowed St Emilion. Joyful wine worth the money.

8 **Wakefield Estate Shiraz 2002**   £7.99
Lavishly spiced and vanilla-toned smoothie with long-lingering flavours, worthy of a special carnivorous occasion.

5 **Wakefield Promised Land Cabernet Merlot 2002**   £5.99
Don't be fooled by the cute seahorse label; this is an overcooked confection to be avoided.

CHILE

10 **Cono Sur Pinot Noir 2003**   £5.03
Close your eyes and you could be sniffing a good village burgundy – the earthy, strawberry aromas are a treat. Even the colour has the slightly weedy look of burgundy, but of course you get much more plump fruit than you would from the old country, especially at this price. A brilliant contrivance.

9 **Casillero del Diablo Shiraz 2002**   £5.49
There's a likable roasted edge to the fruit of this generous and well-balanced wine. It's hefty (and 14% alcohol) but with an elegant weight and nice spicy aftertaste.

FRANCE

9 **La Cuvée Mythique 2001**   £6.49
Ubiquitous Languedoc oaked-aged brand is very dark, with gripping soft tannin and well matched red-berry/black-berry flavours; good weight (13.5% alcohol) and lingering lush flavours. I even like the owly label.

Somerfield

FRANCE

8   **Beaumes de Venise Côtes du Rhône 2001**   £5.79

Monster red (14.5% alcohol) from a village better known for sweet muscat has a toothsome liquorice centre to the spicy-rich fruit and will go well with strongly seasoned dishes.

8   **Château Fonbagan 2001**   £8.49

Impressively dark St Emilion satellite (Puisseguin) is still quite tough with tannin but showing signs of turning into a fine, generous claret. Probably worth the money, but don't drink before 2006.

ITALY

8   **Leonardo Chianti 2003**   £5.99

A well-drawn wine, can one say? The label incorporates the artist's self-portrait and the bottle looks fun. It's 100 per cent Sangiovese, so not the usual Chianti recipe, but has plenty of sleek fruit and a good dry finish.

NEW ZEALAND

8   **Oyster Bay Pinot Noir 2002**   £9.99

Typically slinky and minty Kiwi PN at a perfectly fair price for this sort of exciting quality and interest.

S AFRICA

8   **Somerfield South African Limited Release Pinotage 2002**   £5.99

This is a sweetie, typical squishy Pinotage that will go well with cold roast beef – and will even stand up to horseradish.

8   **The Wolftrap Red 2002**   £5.99

Big, sappy, Cabernet-dominated flavours invade all the taste buds. A ripe, sunny, red-meat sort of wine.

8 Goats du Roam in Villages 2002 £6.99
Winemaker and goat farmer Charles Back aims to make
Rhône-style wines in the Cape, and enjoys annoying the
French with names imitating those of their sacred
appellations. This very dark red has intensity and
spiciness, might be just a little stewed (14% alcohol) and
is good, hearty fun. A step up from standard bestseller
Goats du Roam.

7 Porcupine Ridge Syrah 2002 £6.99
Decent, hearty oaked red at 14.5% alcohol is not as
attention-grabbing as the Sauvignon Blanc made under
this fun label.

8 Somerfield Viña Caña Rioja Reserva 1998 £6.99
Smells of old-fashioned garden roses and vanilla from
this light but elegantly flavoursome mature classic Rioja
at an unusually reasonable price.

8 Delicato Shiraz 2002 £5.99
I wouldn't call it delicate, but a decent spicy
middleweight with easy appeal.

PINK WINES	UNDER £5

7 La Palma Rosé 2004 £4.99
Bright-coloured, straight Merlot-Cabernet blend has
hedgerow whiff and dry, crisp fruitiness.

8 Côte Sauvage Cinsault Rosé 2003 £3.99
Sunny vin de pays d'Oc has a pale magenta colour and
aromas of cherry and toffee. Likable consistent fruit.

S AFRICA

SPAIN

USA

CHILE

FRANCE

PINK WINES   £5 PLUS

9   Fetzer Valley Oaks Syrah Rosé 2003   £5.99
USA
This is as good as rosé needs to get. Shocking pink colour, a perky fleshy wine that shines with the flavours of summer fruit. Well worth paying the extra for. Screwcap.

WHITE WINES   UNDER £5

10   Argento Chardonnay 2003   £4.99
I just cannot fault this consistently brilliant bargain from top producer Catena. It has inviting yellow colour, a theatrically elevated nose, big apple-strudel style and nifty crisp finish. Cheap at the price.

ARGENTINA

8   Somerfield Argentine Chardonnay 2003   £3.99
Nice blanched-almondy style to the fruit in this crisp-finishing good-value bottle made by ubiquitous winemaker Peter Bright.

8   Somerfield First Flight Dry White   £2.99
Aussie wines are a rarity at this price, and this non-vintage one is pretty good in a fresh, limey sort of way.

AUSTRALIA

**8   Somerfield First Flight Colombard
Chardonnay 2002   £3.49**
'Cabbage and citrus', it says on the note I made on the smell of this cheapie, so it must be true. I also wrote, 'Really quite good and fresh at the price, and deserves trying'.

AUSTRALIA

8 **Tortoiseshell Bay Semillon Sauvignon 2003** £3.99
Scent of fresh pineapple and peach-melon fleshy flavours, all amounting to a lot of fun and flavour for the price.

CHILE

8 **Missiones de Rengo Chardonnay 2003** £4.99
Straightforward balanced apple-milky wine that improved quite remarkably on retasting next day, as if the flavours bloomed and intensified with a little oxidation. Try this at home!

9 **Somerfield Domaine du Bois Viognier 2002** £4.99
Soft but fresh Languedoc dry white is a real all-purpose wine. In a blind tasting at my newspaper, it came first, ahead of whites costing more than twice the price. Try it!

FRANCE

8 **Kiwi Cuvée Chardonnay Viognier 2003** £4.99
Plenty of liveliness and interest in this vin de pays d'Oc – though hardly a blend they would make in New Zealand.

7 **Domaine Sainte Agathe Chardonnay 2002** £4.99
Rich colour and plenty of rich appley whiff but a little flat in flavour. Previous vintages have been more exciting, and perhaps the 2003 will be too.

7 **Kiwi Cuvée Sauvignon Blanc 2003** £4.49
It's from the Loire – natural home of the Sauvignon – but made by a New Zealander. It delivers about as much interest as you would expect at the price. Screwcap.

10 **Somerfield German Dry Riesling 2002** £3.99

A very lively little number almost fizzing with fresh, appley vigour. This is quite simply everything an 'everyday' Riesling should be, and it is perfectly delicious. Screwcap.

9 **Gau Biekelheimer Kurfürstenstück Auslese 2003** £3.99

Pale and softly ripe Rheinhessen wine with honey notes and a fine autumnal lushness. Very good at this price, to drink as either an aperitif or as a gently sweet pudding wine. It's 10.5% alcohol.

9 **Kendermanns Riesling Kabinett 2003** £4.29

Cool, appley style to a fresh, dry white from a great German vintage that is refreshing both in itself and in the sense that it has such an uncontrived pure flavour. Just 8.5% alcohol.

9 **Kendermanns Pinot Grigio 2003** £4.53

Brilliant new vintage of this popular Rheinhessen brand, perhaps reflecting the fantastic ripening conditions enjoyed in the Rhine in the best summer since the 1870s. Lush, zingy, smoky fruit with dimension.

8 **Orvieto Classico Cardetto 2003** £4.79

Interesting herbaceous green-fruit style to this delicate dry white from Umbria's tourist-trap hill town of Orvieto. Good aperitif.

8 **Inycon Chardonnay 2003** £4.99

A yellow wine from Sicily with a big new-mown-hay whiff and flavours I thought reminded me of boiled egg and buttered soldiers. At the time, anyway. Hope this does not put anyone off a perfectly decent wine.

8 **Trulli Chardonnay del Salento 2003** £4.99

ITALY

Extravagant yellow colour, and the nose on this southern Italian heavyweight isn't exactly retroussé either. Lots of flavour for your money and a match for most of the Aussie competition.

9 **Boland Cellar Sauvignon Blanc 2003** £4.99

S AFRICA

Cape Sauvignons are now nudging their New Zealand counterparts for quality, and they are already ahead for value. This has a zingy aroma and tons of lively grassy-nettly fruit. Excellent buy.

8 **Danie de Wet Chardonnay Sur Lie 2004** £4.49

Keen-edged bargain with stony-fresh fruit and a keen price, too.

8 **Leaping Horse Chardonnay 2002** £4.99

USA

Richly coloured, with corresponding fruit, balanced by edgy citrus acidity – very good fish wine.

WHITE WINES **£5 PLUS**

10 **Lindemans Coonawarra Botrytis Riesling 1999** £5.99

AUSTRALIA

Gorgeous, gold-coloured sweet wine really does have the ambrosial qualities of botrytis, and there is perfect balancing citrus acidity, too, to give a bright clean edge to the luscious aftertaste. It's the pud wine bargain of the year. Note just 9% alcohol.

8 **Campbells Rutherglen Muscat half bottle** £7.49

Mildly fortified (17.5% alcohol) wine has the mahogany colour of oloroso sherry, a delectable roasted muscat nose and thrilling crème brûlée flavours. A lavish treat to enjoy cool as an aperitif or after dinner, like port.

9 Georges Désire Oak Aged Burgundy 2002 £5.99

This is really good – a rich 'buttery' style with underlying citrus, even brassica, and a useful introduction to one of the world's great wine styles, without breaking the bank.

9 Georges Désire Saint Véran 2002 £6.99

This lovely Maconnais positively glitters with ripe Chardonnay flavours and stone-fresh minerality. Superbly made, a sort of golden days wine, and worth the price.

8 Michel Laroche Chardonnay 2003 £5.99

Big colour and big fruit, too, in this vin de pays d'Oc – a trustworthy branded wine from Chardonnay king Michel Laroche, who hails from Chablis.

7 Somerfield Chablis 2003 £6.99

A soft and friendly Chablis, but not as exciting as some previous vintages under the Somerfield own label.

9 Montana East Coast Unoaked Chardonnay 2002 £5.99

Although by far the biggest wine producer in New Zealand – the British-owned outfit is said to make more than half the total – Montana seems to turn out better and better products. This is their 'basic' Chardonnay and a lavishly delicious one, too, with glowing colour, pure sunny fruit and the clean minerality that is so much the Kiwi hallmark.

FRANCE

NEW ZEALAND

NEW ZEALAND

9 Montana Marlborough Riesling 2002 £5.99
Exotic dry white with floral bouquet and tropical fruit,
yet with a steely, limey top note to the flavour. This is the
sort of wine that goes so well with tricky menu items
such as salads, asparagus, artichokes and so on.

9 Oyster Bay Sauvignon Blanc 2003 £6.99
Famed dry white is typically zesty, with a distinctive
whiff of grapefruit and concentrated flavours including
asparagus and gooseberry, even a hint of kiwi fruit!
Screwcap.

9 Villa Maria Private Bin Sauvignon Blanc
2003 £7.99
Generously rich Sauvignon with emphatic asparagus
note and a tingling white-pepper twang on the finish.
Great wine, as ever. Screwcap.

S AFRICA

8 Porcupine Ridge Sauvignon Blanc 2003 £5.49
Well-coloured, with fresh and zesty fruit. Not as much
spiky acidity as remembered from the last couple of
vintages, and some drinkers may prefer this.

SPARKLING WINES

FRANCE

9 Somerfield Prince William Blanc de Noirs
Champagne £11.99
Super brioche nose on this obligingly cheap champagne
is followed up by fresh lively fruit. Why pay more?

Tesco

Out of every £10 spent in supermarkets in Britain, £2.70 is spent in Tesco. No other supermarket – or any other kind of retailer – comes near. And Tesco is getting bigger. The business now has 237,000 staff, and that makes it the country's largest private-sector employer. Profits increased by a dizzying 22 per cent in the last financial year, to £1.7 billion. Chief executive Sir Terry Leahy has admitted that 'It is not feasible to keep on growing at that rate' but in the longer term believes it is 'a reasonable aspiration to look for double-digit growth'.

On the wine front, Tesco is certainly the biggest of all retailers, and continues relentlessly to develop its huge range, especially at the upmarket end. I have never come across as many top-class bottles at a single Tesco tasting as I did this year, and a lot of these wines are own-labels or real rarities.

The own-label New Zealand wines stand out. Produced by relatively small-scale growers as well the usual giants, they offer the sort of quality that easily matches the well-known brands, and at competitive prices.

A few of the wines listed here are on sale only in Tesco's very biggest branches or in the 25 'Wine Adviser' stores, which – inevitably – are mostly in London and the Home Counties. For the record, they are in: Amersham, Baldock, Bishops Stortford, Blackpool Clifton, Bournemouth, Burgess Hill, Calais, Cheshunt, Colchester, Colney Hatch, Hatfield, Hemel Hempstead, New Malden, Newbury, Newton Abbot, Northampton South, Pitsea, Portsmouth North Harbour, Purley, Romford Gallows Corner, Royston, Saffron Walden, Salisbury, Watford and Winchester.

Bear in mind that any wine you cannot find in a particular store will probably be available online for home delivery at **www.tesco.com**. There is also a new Tesco Wine Direct order-by-phone service, plus the World of Wine, a kind of club operated through the Clubcard loyalty scheme. This, and the online operation, offer all sorts of wines you won't otherwise find in the stores, and sometimes at quite remarkably competitive prices.

RED WINES	UNDER £5

ARGENTINA

9 **Picajuan Peak Bonarda 2003** £3.99
This dark red from the La Agricola-Zuccardi estate contrives to be both softly juicy and keenly edged, in what might be called the Italian style. Screwcap.

CHILE

10 **Casillero del Diablo Cabernet Sauvignon 2002** £3.99
This 'Cellar of the Devil' range from Concha y Toro, Chile's biggest wine-producer, has been around for ages but has just lately bloomed into the most amazing collection of bargains. This Cabernet is fabulous for the price, impressively dark and dense with keen blackcurrant nose, lush with cassis fruit and a hint of chocolate in the depths, and completely satisfying in weight and balance.

ITALY

8 **Tesco Finest Aglianico Basilicata 2002** £4.99
Typical southern Italian red with a cheerful pungency, super-ripe fruit and a hint of sunburn. From Aglianico grapes grown in the volcanic terrain of Monte Vulture.

S AFRICA

9 **Forrester's Petit Pinotage 2003** £4.99
Lollipop nose on this sweetie of a wine – a friendly squashed-summer-fruit glugger that is without fault. Definitely recommended.

ARGENTINA

9 **Catena Cabernet Sauvignon 2001** **£9.99**
It's the sheer sublime purity of this perennial classic that first strikes me, giving welcome meaning to the term 'expressive of the grape variety'. This is how Cabernet Sauvignon would always taste in the best of all possible worlds. This vintage will undoubtedly develop in the bottle for at least a decade. The Catena family is Argentina's leading wine dynasty. Available in Wine Adviser stores only.

9 **Familia Zuccardi Q Tempranillo 2001** **£9.99**
This is like Rioja but with a lot more guts. It's purple-black, extraordinarily concentrated and yet with an ethereal delicacy of body (that's the Rioja-like bit) that makes it intriguingly uplifting as well as downright delicious. The Zuccardis are another of Argentina's great winemaking dynasties (see Catena, immediately above), producing great wines at all levels – including Tesco's own 'Picajuan Peak' range.

AUSTRALIA

8 **Tempus Two Merlot 2002** **£5.03**
Soft, ripe, simple red, with colour going prematurely orange, but perfectly pleasant and 13.5% alcohol.

8 **Oxford Landing Shiraz 2002** **£5.53**
Interesting stalky, green whiff off this dark, hedgerow fruit monster (14% alcohol) and an underlying liquorice note. Firm, young wine to match meaty dishes.

8 **Wolf Blass Yellow Label Cabernet Sauvignon 2002** **£7.53**
Amiable big-brand wine is consistently good, with this vintage delivering rich flavours with breadth and depth. A safe buy.

9 **Tyrrells Old Winery Pinot Noir 2002**   £5.49
Quite pale in colour, this has a nose of alluring cherry and strawberry sweetness, and a well-concentrated middleweight style. Special quality at the price – which is a conditional one, because you have to buy a minimum of six bottles (at £32.94) from the World of Wine Direct online service. The wine is not sold in the stores – more's the pity.

9 **Tesco Australian Howcroft Vineyards**
Cabernet Merlot 2002   £7.99
This own-label red has the edge over most of the well known brands alongside it with its excitingly defined spicy fruit – all delivered in a seductively smooth medium. Dark and dense, it will surely develop until 2007 or maybe longer. It has a screwcap, so you can store it standing up if you like.

9 **Tempus Two Pewter Label Merlot 2002**   £10.03
Black-purple young monster (14% alcohol) with deliciously slurpy classic morello-cherry Merlot fruit is nevertheless subtle and elegant in its way – as much Bordeaux in style as Barossa. Don't be put off by the naff pewter-style label.

9 **Casillero del Diablo Carmenère 2003**   £5.03
Another really cracking wine from this range (see the Cabernet Sauvignon in under-£5 listing above), this is near-black in colour, 14% alcohol and yet has a light touch, beguiling softness and a long, lip-smacking finish. Bargain.

9 **Errazuriz Shiraz 2002**   £5.99
Dark and densely coloured young wine has rich cassis-like fruit with noticeable spiciness and complexity. Lots of class, and good with meaty dishes.

CHILE

9 Louis Felipe Edwards Estate Cabernet Sauvignon 2001 £6.03

Spirity, pruny aroma from this hefty (14% alcohol) red is followed up by a mellow and even velvety fruit with reasonably discreet oak vanilla. A beguiling, luxury wine at a good price.

8 Cono Sur Reserve Pinot Noir 2001 £7.03

A softened version of the excellent standard Cono Sur Pinot Noir, this has beguiling, warm, soft-fruit flavours and is just about worth the extra money.

FRANCE

9 Mont Tauch Fitou Vieilles Vignes 2002 £6.99

Beautifully weighted, oaked luxury Languedoc is supple, spicy, robust, intense and satisfying. Very well made red from the co-operative that first put Fitou on the map.

9 Les Hauts de L'Enclos des Bories La Livinière 2001 £8.03

Top-quality Languedoc – from the tiny Minervois La Livinière appellation – has big spicy flavours (and 'scents of dark prunes, very ripe morello cherries, truffle, cocoa, white pepper and cloves' says Tesco) and satisfying depths. Self-evidently special wine to drink with roast lamb or cassoulet.

8 Tesco Finest Côtes du Rhône Villages Reserve 2002 £5.53

Colour is quite pale and going orange, but this is a good, firm wine with sun-scorched fruit and a pleasing balance of cool mintiness.

8 Beaumes de Venise Côtes du Rhône Villages
2003 £7.25

The village of Beaumes de Venise in the southern Rhône valley is best known for sticky dessert wines made from muscat grapes, but here is a robust young red, purple in colour, packed with spicy black fruit and distinctly tannic. Should be just right in 2005.

8 Clos de Fontedit Les Flacons 2001 £9.99

Languedoc-Roussillon wine with wild colour, massive juicy fruit (14.5% alcohol) and more than a hint of pepper (hallmark of Syrah, the main grape in this) is really for keeping – up to ten years, Tesco says. I am sure it will do amazing things.

8 Louis Jadot Beaune 1er Cru 1998 £14.49

Lovely beckoning cherry nose on this mature village burgundy, which is just beginning to turn burnt orange in colour and has cool, rich classic Pinot Noir fruit that will continue to develop. Online, you can buy a case of six bottles for £59.94 – and that's a very good price indeed, scoring close to 10 points.

7 Castello di Fonterutoli Chianti Classico
1999 £24.99

Incredible price for this very chi-chi Chianti makes it of largely academic interest, but it is quite delicious, with the classic rich cherry smell, dense and poised black fruit and a good tannic grip. Fabulous of its kind, but typically overpriced, too. Wine Adviser stores.

FRANCE

ITALY

9 **Tesco Finest Marlborough Pinot Noir 2002** £10.03

These Tesco own-label Kiwi wines are a sensation. This is a slinky, minty number with lavish plump summer fruit, and at a very fair price for what is. Screwcap.

9 **Tesco Finest Touriga Nacional 2003** £5.99

Artfully contrived black-as-night table wine from the great grape variety of the port business, this has a porty aroma with intriguing nuances of honeycomb and cloves, even meringue. Great stuff that will probably improve in the bottle for years.

10 **Leopards Leap The Lookout Red 2002** £5.03

Bumper whiff off this rather complicated grape blend (mainly Shiraz, Pinotage and Merlot) suggests all sorts of things including blackberries, cinnamon and highway-hot tyres. Weight is modest but concentration is tight and the flavours rewardingly complex. Terrific buy at this price.

8 **Goats du Roam in Villages 2002** £7.03

Winemaker and goat farmer Charles Black aims to make Rhône-style wines in the Cape, and enjoys annoying the French with names imitating those of their sacred appellations. This very dark red has intensity and spiciness, might be just a little stewed (14% alcohol) and is good hearty fun – a step up from standard bestseller Goats do Roam.

Pink Wines   £5 Plus

USA

🍷9   **Fetzer Valley Oaks Syrah Rosé 2003**   £5.98
This is as good as rosé needs to get. Shocking pink colour,
a perky, fleshy wine that shines with the flavours of
summer fruit. Well worth paying the extra for. Screwcap.

White Wines   Under £5

CHILE

🍷8   **Tesco Finest Chilean Sauvignon Blanc**
2003   £3.99
Positive grassy nose and nice brisk fruit with more than
a hint of asparagus in the middle flavour. Good
workaday Sauvignon at a keen price.

GERMANY

🍷8   **Tesco Finest Mosel Riesling QbA 2003**   £4.99
Pleasant, straight fresh Riesling with undercurrent of
honey finishes dry and clean. Modest 10.5% alcohol.

HUNGARY

🍷9   **Tesco Simply Gewürztraminer**   £3.53
From our new EU partner, a really lovable Gewürz with
proper grapefruit-lychee whiff and lots of lush, smoky-
spicy fruit. Just right for sweetness, too, finishing up
brisk and clean. Clever stuff.

ITALY

🍷7   **Tesco Finest Grillo 2003**   £4.99
Highly coloured wine from Sicily's native Grillo grape is
strong (13.5% alcohol) and dry with a sappy sort of
style that will provide interest and refreshment with
tricky dishes such as oily fish.

S AFRICA

🍷8 **Graham Beck Waterside White 2003** £3.53
It's white but it's not watery – and it's very cheap. A crisp little wine, mostly Chardonnay, with plenty of middle flavour.

SPAIN

🍷9 **Torres Viña Sol 2003** £4.38
Cracking new vintage of this constant dry white from Spain's best winemaker, Miguel Torres. It's wholly un-Spanish, in an aromatic style reminiscent of the best kind of Alsace Pinot Blanc, as sunny and refreshing as it sounds.

USA

🍷8 **Tesco Californian Viognier 2002** £3.99
Soft, obliging little wine with the preserved-fruit (apricot, peach) style that suggests the Viognier grape. Jolly likable wine for the money.

🍷7 **Tesco Finest Reserve Californian Chardonnay 2002** £4.99
'Banana, melon and pear aromas' are claimed for this muscular (14.5% alcohol) Californian rippler, but I liked it for its rather farmyardy flavour and persistent finish.

WHITE WINES	£5 PLUS

AUSTRALIA

🍷9 **Oxford Landing Sauvignon Blanc 2003** £5.03
This big brand surprises me year after year by coming up consistently with one of Australia's best-value Sauvignons. This vintage is nettle-fresh with plenty of agreeably green fruit and a lifting lemony finish. Just 11.5% alcohol and in a screwcap bottle.

9 **Tesco Denman Vineyard Hunter Semillon 2002** £7.99

Quite a tangy Semillon with typical pineapple, banana and citrus notes, and a very nifty balance of all this exotic stuff with a crisp, zealous acidity. A cracking wine, distinctive and rewarding, and note just 11% alcohol. Screwcap.

9 **Tim Adams Clare Valley Semillon 2001** £8.03

Old-fashioned yellow wine with spirity pineapple-banana nose, jumbo flavours of fruit salad and an arresting acidity. This wine really does sing, and it affirms that Australia can do great things outside the Chardonnay arena.

8 **Tesco Finest Great Southern Riesling 2003** £6.03

Big limey wine in the classic Aussie manner with long, long flavour – a food wine to go with anything fishy or creamy. Screwcap.

8 **Wolf Blass Yellow Label Chardonnay 2003** £7.53

Lots of colour and a creamy vanilla whiff from this popular luxury brand. It's not exactly subtle, but I like the big butterscotch flavour, trimmed up with a well contrived acidity. Screwcap.

8 **Tesco Denman Vineyard Hunter Chardonnay 2002** £7.99

Rich yellow colour – and yellow flavours, too, as in the maker's own description of 'hints of peach and supple vanilla perfume coupled with a toasty French oak'. Screwcap.

AUSTRALIA

🍷 8 Tempus Two Pewter Label Chardonnay 2003 £10.03

Looks a bit of a novelty wine in its odd, lozenge-shaped bottle and with the 'pewter-style' metallised embossed paper label, but actually it's brilliant stuff, with a stony-but-lush burgundy-style nose and heaps of lush mineral-apple fruit, and undertones of toffee and caramel. Balanced and well made – and rather fun.

🍷 7 Firefinch Sauvignon Blanc 2003 £5.03

Notably complex, inviting, floral nose leads into an agreeably vigorous fruitiness that suffers just a shade from flabbiness at the finish.

🍷 10 Tesco Finest Alsace Gewürztraminer 2002 £7.03

This is what great own-label wines should be about. Tesco have gone to some Alsace producer I've never heard of called Kuehn, and found this simply perfect Gewürz. It's a deep gold colour and has a rich, impossibly complex, spicy nose, suggesting spectacular ripeness, and a corresponding panorama of classic flavours. The finish is textbook clean – not a hint of the excess residual sugar that spoils far too many much costlier Alsace Gewürzes. Even the label, with its elaborate, wordy illuminated-manuscript theme, is rather fun. Top wine.

🍷 9 Château Suduiraut 1999 half bottle £22.01

Spectacular sweet wine from one of the great 'premier cru' estates of Sauternes is an unexpected supermarket find. The price might seem incredible but is par for the course for a world-famous estate like this in a good year. Wine Adviser stores only.

8 **Touraine Sauvignon Domaine des Loges 2003** £5.03

Smooth sort of Loire Sauvignon has alluring grapefruity nose and plenty of classic grassy flavour. Very easy to drink.

8 **Blason de Bourgogne Saint Véran 2001** £8.03

From the Maconnais district of Burgundy, this has a marvellously inviting smell – I wrote down buttery scrambled egg, cream and apples – and an equally appealing range of layered flavours. Fresh yet complex, flavoursome yet elegant. Ready to drink but might well develop.

8 **Blason de Bourgogne Pouilly-Fuissé 2003** £10.99

Grand, assertive Maconnais with minerality and punchy fruit, and memorable purity of style. A famous appellation on good form, and, yes, worth the money.

8 **Sancerre Domaine de la Villaudière 2003** £11.03

Brisk gooseberry nose on this classic, expensive Loire Sauvignon is followed up by layered flavours and fascinating brassica notes. If it just has to be Sancerre, this is a very good one. Available only in the 25 'Wine Adviser' stores.

8 **Tesco Finest Sauternes 2001 half bottle** £12.01

Extravagantly rich pud wine of evident quality though indistinct origin (it is from the 'Producer's Club' of giant Bordeaux dealer-winemaker Yvon Mau) has a perfect clean finish and is genuinely worth the money.

7 **Tesco Finest Picpoul de Pinet 2003** £5.03

I am convinced Picpoul de Pinet owes 90 per cent of its popularity to its weird name, but this decent, hefty dry white from near Caracassonne in the Languedoc has merit enough in its own right. Screwcap.

FRANCE

**H de l'Hospitalet White Vin de Pays d'Oc
2002** £6.99
A substantial dry white from two-thirds Chardonnay
and one of Viognier and Sauvignon makes for a woody
blend, with firm flavours of apples, pears and other more
mysterious allusions. Assertive, appealing wine. Much
cheaper (scoring 8) online, at £29.94 for six bottles.

 **Tesco Finest Chablis Grand Cru
Les Bouguerots 2001** £22.03
I include this just for academic interest. Made by the
great Michel Laroche, it's your richer style of Chablis
with flashes of flintiness, and very fine indeed. The price
is outrageous – and the bottle has a screwcap, which
certainly scores for radical chic.

 Guigal Condrieu 2001 £23.03
Sinfully delicious Rhône Valley classic was once the only
source of wine from the Viognier grape. If you're rich
enough and curious enough to try the model for today's
ocean of New World and regional French Viognier, this
will be an experience. Wine Advisor stores only.

Tesco Finest Pinot Grigio 2003 £6.99
Ultra-zesty nose on this top-quality PG progresses to a
substantial, lively fruitiness positively prickling with
smoky, spicy, fruit-basket flavours. From the Friuli region
in north-east Italy but made by a New Zealander – which
might explain a lot about the liveliness of this terrific wine.

ITALY

🍷 9   Ca' Dei Frati Lugana 2002   £8.99

I think it's brave of Tesco to persist with pricy Italian white wines, because there is a common view among the cognoscenti that all *vino blanco* is boring and pointless. This one isn't. It comes in a frightfully smart bottle, is a gorgeous lemon-gold colour and has a seductive peach-blossom nose, and amidst the vigorous, fleshy-but-mineral fruit there's a dash of richness that put me in mind of buttered crumpets. Special.

🍷 8   Tesco Finest Gavi 2003   £5.99

Luxury Italian dry white from the Piedmont region has exotic appeal with a near-spirity nose, lush, herbaceous fruit and a notably lemony finish. Makes a rather grand aperitif wine.

NEW ZEALAND

🍷 10   Tesco Finest Marlborough Sauvignon Blanc 2003   £7.49

Superb. Sea-breeze nose with beach-grass and asparagus elements gives it thrilling appeal. In the mouth, it has the same perfect poise – classic Sauvignon with that inimitable rasping quality and in its depths, a fleeting hint of sweetness. Simply gorgeous, and unmatched at this price. Screwcap.

🍷 9   Tesco Finest Hawkes Bay Chardonnay 2002   £7.49

Luminous lemon-gold colour and a generous sweet-apple nose on this extravagant ripe-but-pebbly-crisp Kiwi classic, made by dependable Montana.

PORTUGAL

🍷 9   Tesco Finest 10-Year-Old Tawny Port   £11.04

Made for Tesco by the ubiquitous Symington family under their Smith Woodhouse name, this is a good, copper-coloured, wood-aged port offering an exciting blend of fruit and fire with dimensions of flavour that make the price look very fair.

S AFRICA

9 **Thelema Sauvignon Blanc 2003** £12.53
Fabulous wine, as it needs to be at the price, this offers a real focus of classic Sauvignon aroma and flavour and is a great treat. Thelema is one of the Cape's greatest producers, and this is certainly a wine I would drink if I could afford it.

7 **Firefinch Sauvignon Blanc 2003** £5.03
Notably complex, inviting floral nose leads into an agreeably vigorous fruitiness that suffers just a shade from flabbiness at the finish.

10 **Tesco Finest Oloroso Sherry** £5.04
Amber-mahogany colour, toasty-nutty nose and sublime fruit in this dry, perfectly made sherry at a giveaway price. In a small glass, drink it cool as an autumnal aperitif with nuts or tapas, or at room temperature with cheese as an exotic end to a meal.

SPAIN

9 **Tesco Finest Manzanilla Sherry** £5.03
Bone-dry pale sherry is very good indeed. The brisk, briny aroma fairly jumps at you from the glass, and the fruit is tangy and ultra-fresh – the best aperitif in the world, bar none. These dry sherries, the kind the Spanish themselves drink, need to be served well chilled in a small white-wine glass. They keep fresh for no longer than white table wine, and are only about 15% alcohol.

9 **Torres Viña Esmeralda 2003** £6.03
A dry but exotic white from the Torres winery in Penedes near Barcelona, with intriguing aromas of grapefruit, pineapple and melon, it delivers a correspondingly delicious basketful of fresh fruit flavours. A marvellous and unique wine, from Moscatel and Gewürztraminer. Screwcap.

USA

**7 Ravenswood Vintners Blend Chardonnay
2001**   £7.03
Plenty of peach and vanilla in this well known brand
from California's Sonoma Valley make it plush and
relishable, and I like the sherbet note at the edge of the
flavour.

Waitrose

Waitrose is on the move. In 2004 it has expanded its network from 144 stores to 163 by buying 19 supermarkets from Morrisons, who were obliged to dispose of newly acquired Safeway outlets so close to their own existing outlets it could threaten consumer choice.

As a result, Waitrose will have branches as far north as Lincoln, Sheffield and Harrogate, and others in Wales to supplement their current single store in the principality at Monmouth.

High street wine merchants in these places will not be among those celebrating these new arrivals, because Waitrose is a formidable competitor. Their wine list is far and away the best of any supermarket chain, and despite Waitrose's reputation – wholly unwarranted, I believe – as an expensive place to shop, the wines are very keenly priced indeed.

There are great numbers of excellent wines at under a fiver, and Waitrose has a monthly programme of promotional pricing that makes discounted wines a perpetual feature of the well laid out wine departments.

From 2005, millions more shoppers will be living within reasonable distance of a Waitrose, and for others there will still be the home-delivery service, Waitrose Direct Wines, available to all. For a copy of the list, and delivery details, ring 0800 188881 or log on to **www.waitrose.com/wines**.

RED WINES   UNDER £5

AUSTRALIA

8 **Tatachilla Growers Grenache-Mourvèdre-Shiraz 2003**   **£4.99**
Dark, seductively juicy bargain from a rightly respected producer.

7 **Bear Crossing Shiraz-Merlot 2003**   **£4.99**
Raisiny red by Angove's with plenty of interest. Koala lovers need not fear disappointment.

10 **Cono Sur Pinot Noir 2003**   **£4.99**
Close your eyes and you could be sniffing a good village burgundy – the earthy, strawberry aromas are a treat. Even the colour has the slightly weedy look of burgundy, but of course you get much more plump fruit than you would from the old country, especially at this price. A brilliant contrivance.

CHILE

9 **Traidcraft Los Robles Carmenère 2003**   **£4.99**
Interesting vine-stalk whiff within the ripe berry smell of this Fair Trade wine, which has lush pure fruit all the way through. Very good buy, making it no hardship to support the Fair Trade scheme, employing people in the developing world at fair wages.

8 **San Andrés Carmenère/Cabernet Sauvignon 2003**   **£3.99**
Nice hedgerow-fruit cheapie has simple appeal but lots of interest – fruit syrup style but by no means oversweet. Great everyday red.

10 **La Rectorie Côtes du Ventoux 2003** **£3.99**
Evocative new-squished fruit aromas and flavours from this generous and gripping Rhône red that combines vivacity and length in its brilliantly contrived fruit. Outstanding 'everyday' wine in a screwcap bottle.

9 **Cuvée Chasseur 2003** **£2.99**
Can't fault this very cheap vin de pays de l'Hérault, with cheery brambly smell and flavour that goes all the way through.

9 **Waitrose Côtes du Rhône 2003** **£3.99**
Perfectly ripe red with dense colour, a hint of raisin on the nose and lots of sunshine in the bold, spicy fruit. Screwcap.

9 **La Colombe Côtes du Rhône 2003** **£4.99**
Big-flavoured, minty-peppery purply red with vigour and depth.

8 **Fruits of France Grenache 2002** **£3.99**
Plenty of weight and concentration in this vin de pays d'Oc, with long and satisfying fruit. Juicy and spicy. Screwcap.

8 **Waitrose Good Ordinary Claret 2002** **£4.29**
Definitely good but hardly ordinary, this tastes well above what I normally expect to find from Bordeaux at this sort of price.

8 **Saumur Les Nivières 2002** **£4.49**
Pale, leafy-smelling, lightweight and slightly under ripe Loire red is, honestly, good of its kind.

FRANCE

FRANCE

8 **La Chasse Du Pape Syrah 2003** £4.99

Impressive dense purple colour, sweet briary nose and fruit, with adhesive tannin. A food wine with spice and grip, this is a big-brand vin de pays d'Oc worth buying.

7 **Cahors 2002** £4.59

Sweet-smelling, tough-tasting, high acid red from an appellation that rarely produces anything interesting. I know many people admire Cahors, including this one, so include it here to show how open-minded I am.

ITALY

8 **Inycon Shiraz 2002** £4.99

This stylish Sicilian brand is a bit up and down, but this hefty (14% alcohol) baked-fruit red is generous and lingering in flavour.

8 **Tarantino Da Luca Primitivo-Merlot 2002** £4.99

Chunky dark wine from Puglia with easy appeal has a softer centre than straight Primitivo reds. Artfully made.

8 **Montepulciano d'Abruzzo, Umani Ronchi, 2002** £4.49

Rightly popular style of brambly, eager spaghetti wine with cherry notes and brisk dry finish.

PORTUGAL

8 **Altano Douro 2001** £4.49

A jolly red made from the port country – the Douro Valley – this bears more than a passing resemblance to the style. Juicy and fun, it's made by the Symington family, who own half the top port brands.

S AFRICA

7 **Graham Beck Railroad Red 2003** £4.99

Brambly young red with hints of raisin and consistent flavour.

SPAIN

8 Don Hugo Vino de la Tierra Manchuela   £3.49
Thoroughly plausible plonk from the Spanish wine-lake region of La Mancha, this non-vintage wine has a mature-looking, vanilla-oak nose and soft cherry-blackcurrant fruit. Really rather good.

RED WINES   UNDER £5

**9 Henschke Keyneton Estate
Shiraz-Cabernet-Merlot 2000   £18.50**
Sumptuous sweet top note on the smell is the perfect intro to this fabulous wine from one of Australia's most revered producers. Expensive, yes, but this is world class, and an experience.

8 Deakin Estate Merlot 2002   £6.99
I remember when this brand from the state of Victoria was just about the cheapest good-quality wine from anywhere in Australia. The prices have gone up a lot, but the quality has held up too, making for a rather sophisticated Merlot with long, concentrated fruit.

8 Peter Lehmann Clancy's Red 2002   £6.99
Solid, dimensional Shiraz-Cabernet-Merlot blend with plenty of ripe fruit and grip.

8 D'Ahrenberg Footbolt Shiraz 2001   £7.99
Big mouthfilling red with agricultural appeal.

**8 Penfolds Organic Cabernet-Merlot-Shiraz
2002   £9.29**
Surprisingly austere on first taste, this is in the 'cool climate' style of Bordeaux, but the weight of ripeness (and 14.5% alcohol) soon makes its presence felt. Lovely stuff.

AUSTRALIA

CHILE

8 **Mont Gras Cabernet Sauvignon Syrah Reserva 2002** £6.99

Very agreeable pure-fruit style of wine with a lot of alcohol (14.5%) and subtle, velvety oak influence but with crisp clean fruit.

10 **Château Villepreux 2002** £5.49

I liked this so much at the tasting I bought half a dozen to have with my birthday tea, where everyone raved about it. Very dense colour with corresponding ripe plummy nose, generous fruit with endearing plumpness and just the right grip of tannin. Outstanding claret among several very good ones at Waitrose.

9 **Waitrose Special Reserve Claret 2002** £5.29

Lots of mint and liquorice in this substantial and gripping Bordeaux to drink now or keep a year or two in confident expectations of development.

FRANCE

9 **Château La Varière Cuvée Jacques Beaujeu 2002** £7.99

Dark, firmly blackberryish but deliciously supple Loire wine specially made for Waitrose is genuinely characterful.

9 **Château Segonzac 2002** £7.99

Dense ruby colour and a figgy nose on this plumptious Côtes de Blaye (Bordeaux) that has masses of ripe 'upfront' fruit. Drinking very well already.

9 **Les Vieilles Vignes de Château Maris 2002** £7.99

Intense luxury oaked Minervois is a mature smoothie that will have broad appeal as a special occasion winter red. With 14% alcohol.

FRANCE

9   **Château La Fleur Chambeau 2001**   £8.69
Mature, richly textured claret from Lussac-St-Emilion has dark cassis fruit and ideal weight – yet another terrific Bordeaux buy.

9   **Mercurey 1er Cru Les Puillets,**
      Château Philippe-le-Hardi 2001   £11.99
Classic earthy burgundy has pale brown-orange colour, a faintly spirity whiff with intense strawberry notes and gloriously sunny ripe fruit.

9   **Château Laroque 1999**   £17.49
A St Emilion grand cru of scintillating quality, with silky fruit and plenty of the sort of complexity and dimension you are entitled to expect at this sort of price. A 'prestige' wine actually worth the money.

8   **Bourgogne Pinot Noir, J-C Boisset 2001**   £5.99
Pale and already going orangey-brown, this rustic burgundy is very likeable, with soft strawberry fruit and a warming hint of spice.

8   **Château Cazal-Viel Cuvée des Fées**
      St-Chinian 2002   £6.99
Grand-tasting, concentrated and eagerly tannic southern red with classic spicy-silky style of the Syrah grape.

8   **Château de Targé, Saumur-Champigny**
      2001   £7.49
Swishy Loire red has a lush strawberry heart to its flavour and the distinctive firmness and lightness of the region's best wines.

GREECE

8 Tsantali Cabernet Sauvignon 2000 £6.49
Scores for curiosity, but a decent wine at this price, indistinguishable, I'd say, from the sort of oaked Cabernet they make in the Languedoc region of France.

ITALY

9 Barolo Monfalletto Cordero di Montezemolo 1999 £25.00
Fantastic wine at a fantastic price. Colour is a gorgeous brick-red mixed with deep copper. The nose is so like that of a very old dry amontillado sherry I did a double-take. Fruit is divine in the classic 'tar and roses' style of Barolo, and if you want to know what this famous style of wine tastes like, splurge the housekeeping on this one, which is drinking very well now.

8 Chianti Classico Borgo Salcetino 2001 £8.99
Chianti does seem to be getting expensive, but if you're willing to fork out, this is very much in character, with sleek redcurrant aroma, rich and weighty fruit and textbook nutskin-dry finish.

8 Villa Antinori 2001 £9.99
Dense and velvety modified Chianti is plush and pleasing – a wine known worldwide, but none the worse for that.

8 Amarone della Valpolicella Classico Vignale 2000 £13.99
Splendid brooding monster made with grapes dried out for a few months after harvest then pressed and fermented to make this unique style of super-concentrated wine, with 15% alcohol. Darkly delicious after-dinner wine good with hard cheeses, particularly spiky ones like Provolone.

ITALY

7   **Barolo Terre da Vino 1999**   **£12.99**

This wine has a fine, glowing copper-ruby colour and the spirity heat that typifies Barolo, finishing very dry. It seems expensive for what it is, but is one of the better Barolos I've tasted during the year.

MEXICO

7   **LA Cetto Petite Sirah 2001**   **£5.25**

Very dark wine from Baja California has raspberry-ripple nose, a grip of tannin, lots of friendly fruit and just a hint of raisiny overripeness, but a properly authentic wine to drink with chilli and tacos.

NEW ZEALAND

9   **Oyster Bay Merlot 2002**   **£7.99**

New Zealand Merlot is still rather a rarity, and this one is rarely delicious – slinky, lush, cool and minty with that rush of pure, mineral fruit unique to the Kiwi method. It's 14% alcohol and comes in a screwcap bottle.

9   **Cloudy Bay Pinot Noir 2002**   **£15.99**

Perfectly poised wine of obvious class just about living up to the world-famous name of Cloudy Bay, whose original blockbusting Sauvignon Blanc has by now been rather eclipsed. This is a fabulous Pinot, well worth the money for the right occasion.

PORTUGAL

8 **Manta Preta 2001** £5.99
Inky-crimson Estremadura red is solid and satisfying with the slinky-glyceriney style that distinguishes so many Portuguese wines.

8 **Dourosa Quinta de la Rosa 2002** £6.99
This posh port-country table wine is quite dry and restrained in fruit and texture but has a sultry middle fruit and lots of aftertaste to make it an intriguingly delicious confection.

8 **Vila Santa JP Ramos 2001** £8.25
Nice plummy-spirity nose on this extravagant oaked red with 14% alcohol and long blackberry flavours.

S AFRICA

10 **Diemersfontein Pinotage 2003** £6.99
Pinotage is the native grape of the Cape, and this wine is an ideal example of a unique style, smelling like blueberry pie fresh from the oven, and yielding up a delicious mélange of flavours. An absolute charmer.

8 **Brampton OVR 2002** £6.99
Sumptuous Cabernet Sauvignon-dominated blend has recognisable blackcurrant aroma and intense but well-balanced fruit. OVR stands for Old Vines Red.

SPAIN

9 **Mas Collet Celler de Capçanes 2001** £6.49
Cassis syrup smell to this very dark, oaked red is followed up by a balanced fruit of elegant weight. Great stuff.

9 **Finca Sobreño Crianza Toro 1999** £7.25
Strong (14.5% alcohol) and well developed, darkly fruity, de luxe red from the Toro region has a leathery grip and spicy intensity. It tastes special because it is special.

SPAIN

🍷8　**Coma Vella Mas d'en Gil Priorat 2000**　£15.99
Gamey, expensive nose on this impossibly dark and dense, black fruit monster from the ultra-fashionable Priorat DO. Huge wine, 14% alcohol, with complexity and depth, it is arguably worth the money.

USA

🍷8　**Bonterra Merlot 2001**　£9.99
Plump black cherry organic wine of assured quality, this is dangerously easy drinking and worth the money.

URUGUAY

🍷8　**Pizzorno Reserve 2002**　£7.99
Dark and muscular yet self-evidently classy red to glug with the reddest of beef.

PINK WINES	UNDER £5

🍷9　**Waitrose Rosé d'Anjou 2003**　£3.99
Pale smoked-salmon colour, floral perfume and lots of charming strawberry-blossomy, soft, fleshy fruit. Just 11.5% alcohol. Great value.

FRANCE

🍷8　**Rosé Cuvée Fleur 2003**　£3.49
Pale pink, simple dry vin de pays with a surprising depth of fruit – plenty of interest for the price.

🍷8　**La Baume Syrah Rosé 2003**　£4.99
Lurid magenta colour and vivid raspberry fruit in this good vin de pays d'Oc.

🍷7　**Rosé Domaine de Pellehaut 2003**　£4.99
Shocking pink Gascony vin de pays has taut and gripping fruit.

ITALY

8 **Cantina di Monteforte Rosato 2003** £3.99
Salmon-pink, straight summer-fruit style with very good dry finish and freshness, from the Soave area of the Veneto.

PINK WINES £5 PLUS

CHILE

10 **Torres San Medin Cabernet Sauvignon Rosé 2003** £5.49
Magenta colour, nose of leafy Cabernet and, as per the claim on the back label, 'plums and cherries over a background of grapefruit' in the flavour. This is my pick of the pinks this year because it's real rosé, not a compromise, with eager flavour.

WHITE WINES UNDER £5

ARGENTINA

9 **La Boca Torrontes-Chardonnay 2003** £3.99
Fun aromatic wine dominated by the dry-Muscat flavours of the Torrontes grape. It's a dry but exotic blend, flavoursome but fresh, and refreshingly cheap.

8 **Finca Las Higueras Pinot Gris 2003** £4.69
Mildly smoky and spicy aromatic dry white with an eye-catching yellow colour.

AUSTRALIA

8 **Bear Crossing Chardonnay 2003** £4.99
Good budget-priced, unoaked wine with heaps of healthy fresh fruit and crisp limey acidity.

CHILE

8 **San Andrés Chardonnay 2003** £3.99
Well formed dry unoaked wine with agreeable peachy style.

CHILE

8 **Casillero del Diablo Chardonnay 2002** £4.99
Cool but generous, straight Chardonnay with notes of tropical fruits.

FRANCE

9 **Cuvée Pêcheur 2003** £3.49
Smell on this deep-south vin de pays suggests the grass and nettles of Sauvignon but is from humbler Ugni Blanc and Colombard grapes – an interesting contrivance, fresh and friendly, and very cheap.

9 **Saumur Les Andides 2002** £4.49
Real bargain, this. Lots of colour and a real liveliness of fruit, with poised acidity and asparagus aftertaste. Fascinating Loire dry white at a giveaway price.

9 **Mâcon-Villages Chardonnay Cave de Prissé 2003** £4.99
Alluring toffee suggestion in the flavour of this friendly, plump-but-crisp burgundy.

8 **Fruits of France Sauvignon Blanc 2003** £3.99
Understated but likeable Languedoc variation on the eternal theme makes for a good fresh everyday dry white.

8 **Waitrose Touraine Sauvignon Blanc 2003** £4.49
A 'medium' dry Loire white with lots of briny scent and a soft but refreshing gooseberry fruitiness.

8 **Saint-Pourçain Réserve Spéciale 2003** £4.69
Pleasing lemon-gold colour and pebble-fresh pong on this Loire dry white, which is full of fresh fruit flavours.

FRANCE

8 **La Baume Viognier 2003** £4.99

Old friend from the Languedoc is as good as ever in this new vintage, and full of the typical apricot flavours of the Viognier grape.

8 **La Chasse du Pape Chardonnay/Viognier 2003** £4.99

This hearty vin de pays d'Oc is generously ripe and fairly priced.

8 **Muscadet sur lie Côtes de Grandlieu Fief Guérin 2003** £4.99

Nice lemony, generously fruity style without too much of the green acidity that's a common failing in Muscadet. Good buy.

HUNGARY

10 **Riverview Gewürztraminer 2003** £3.99

This is brilliant – proper lychee nose and exotic spicy fruit, and (unlike many of the Alsace originals it's trying to imitate) it does not suffer from too much residual sweetness. Great wine to drink as is or with oriental food.

8 **Riverview Sauvignon Blanc 2003** £3.99

Nettly nose and friendly Sauvignon fruit here. Good, fresh bargain.

8 **Nagyréde Estate Chardonnay 2003** £3.79

Brisk dry style is fresh and without fault. Good value.

ITALY

8 **Inycon Chardonnay 2003** £4.99

A yellow wine from Sicily with a big new-mown-hay whiff and flavours I thought reminded me of boiled egg and buttered soldiers. At the time, anyway. Hope this does not put anyone off a perfectly decent wine.

ITALY

8 **Soave Classico Vigneto Colombara Zenato 2003** £4.99
Very fruity, soft-finishing and minty wine of a quality well above average for Soave.

7 **Verdicchio dei Castelli di Jesi Classico 2003** £4.29
Yeasty and flavoursome dry white in an unchallenging style. Screwcap.

S AFRICA

9 **Excelsior Estate Sauvignon Blanc 2003** £4.99
Lush, pure Sauvignon has an extravagant style and lingering aftertaste. Exceptional value.

8 **Cape Grace Sauvignon-Chenin Blanc 2003** £3.99
Fun asparagus note in nose and fruit of this summery, grassy-fresh glugger at a keen price.

8 **Cape Promise Barrel Fermented Chenin Blanc** £4.49
Firm, crisp dry white grabs your tastebuds and delivers lots of flavour.

WHITE WINES £5 PLUS

AUSTRALIA

9 **Terrazas Alto Chardonnay 2003** £5.99
Gold colour, lavish creamy nose and corresponding ripe, balanced apple-pie fruit.

9 **Catena Chardonnay 2002** £9.99
Argentina's benchmark Chardonnay is a perennial masterpiece.

AUSTRALIA

8 **Nepenthe Sauvignon Blanc 2003** £7.99
Lots of liveliness in this zesty, nettly refresher with impressive depths of flavour.

CHILE

8 **Carmen Winemaker's Reserve Chardonnay 2003** £8.99
'Buttery' style to this big, ripe and enticingly lively wine.

FRANCE

10 **Pouilly-Fuissé Vieilles Vignes Château Vitallis 2002** £11.49
Gold-coloured Mâconnais of great character has lashings of toffee-apple fruit and glittering finish. Burgundy at its relatively affordable best.

9 **Domaine Petit Château Chardonnay 2002** £5.59
Particularly sunny and generous, ripe dry vin de pays from the Loire. Refreshing yet intense fruit.

9 **Chablis Caves des Vignerons 2002** £8.49
Amidst lots of poor Chablis tasted in 2004, this stands out. Whopping fruit and lots of mineral interest in the authentic style.

8 **Bourgogne Chardonnay J-C Boisset 2002** £5.99
Healthy mineral whiff and positive notes of grapefruit and pineapple in this sunny dry wine.

8 **Château Saint-Jean-des-Graves 2003** £5.99
Classic, restrained, elegant Bordeaux dry white with nuanced flavours balanced between fleshy-fruit and keen crispness.

FRANCE

8 **La Begude Chardonnay 2001** £6.99
From Limoux in the Pyrenees a richly coloured dry wine with some brassica notes, a lush underlying sweetness and lively edge.

8 **Les Fleurs Chardonnay-Sauvignon 2003** £6.99
Lavish fruity monster from Gascony has really emphatic flavours of both its constituent grape varieties.

8 **Pouilly-Fumé Masson Blondelet 2002** £10.49
Stimulating aroma and fruit from a famed Loire appellation, this is a lovely keen-edged grassy Sauvignon with long, contemplative flavours.

8 **Alsace Pinot Gris Le Fromenteau Josmeyer 2002** £12.99
Arcane but wonderful, aromatic, late-harvest, ripe-but-brisk Alsace wine of great quality.

GERMANY

9 **Ockfener Bockstein Riesling Dr Wagner 2002** £5.99
Zingy moselle QbA with flashes of nectar in the middle flavour and long, long flavours. Superbly weighted dryish wine with just 9% alcohol.

8 **Brauneberger Juffer Riesling Kabinett Willi Haag 2002** £7.99
Fine, floral, young-but-not-green Moselle with heaps of character and 9% alcohol.

NEW ZEALAND

8 **Villa Maria Private Bin Riesling 2003** £6.99
Lovely, big, limey dry white with racy freshness and long flavours.

8 **Jackson Estate Sauvignon Blanc 2003** £8.99
Tangy and yet concentrated exotic flavours in this vivid wine. Screwcap.

PORTUGAL

8 Quinta de Simaens 2003 £5.49
Tangy, dry vinho verde of a superior kind – good enough to revive interest in this once-fashionable wine.

S AFRICA

8 Porcupine Ridge Sauvignon Blanc 2003 £5.99
Amusing name and label, and a wine with plenty of asparagus-tinged fresh fruit with a lively limey finish.

8 Rustenberg Chardonnay 2002 £9.99
Bumper spearmint style to this big golden wine, justifying the price.

SPAIN

10 Hidalgo La Gitana Manzanilla Sherry £6.49
The tangiest, tastiest, pale, bone-dry sherry of them all, from seaside bodega at Sanlucar de Barrameda, is an inimitably great aperitif to drink fresh and chilled.

10 Waitrose Solera Jerezana
Dry Amontillado Sherry £5.99
Superb, aromatic, nutty, dry, copper-coloured sherry at an inexplicably low price. Drink chilled in the warm, and unchilled in the cold.

10 Waitrose Solera Jerezana
Dry Oloroso Sherry £5.99
Deep-amber wine with heaps of raisiny nutty flavours, all in a rich but cleanly dry texture. Very exciting quality for sherry at this sort of price.

9 Palacio de Bornos Verejo Rueda 2003 £5.49
Fresh, nettly dry white with layered flavours has masses of interest and appeal. Seafood wine of great character.

Torres Viña Esmeralda 2003 £5.49

Wonderfully dependable aromatic dry white of terrific character from Muscat and Gewürztraminer grapes. Screwcap bottle and a modest 11% alcohol.

 **Waitrose Solera Jerezana
Rich Cream Sherry** £5.99

Lovely burnt-amber colour and preserved-fruit aroma to a wine in which 'rich cream' means not so much sweet as velvetised, with more than a suggestion of fruit cake.

 **Lustau East India Solera
Rich Oloroso Sherry** £10.99

Conker-coloured, long-aged, sumptuous sherry with nose of burnt toffee and fabulous flavours of preserved fruit. Absolute heaven.

 **Albariño Pazo de Seoane Rias Baixas
2003** £7.99

Quite a bracing first flavour to this zingy and deliciously complex dry white with length and freshness.

Glossary

Wine labels convey a lot of information, some of it useful. Under a combination of UK and EU regulations, the quantity and alcoholic strength of the contents must be displayed, as must the country of origin. And with the exception of the wines from the traditional regions and appellations of France (Bordeaux, Burgundy etc.), Italy (Barolo, Chianti) and Spain (Rioja, Navarra), the label is also very likely to bear the name of the grape or grapes involved. In the mass market, grape names such as Chardonnay and Shiraz now count for a lot more than this or that vineyard, region or even nation.

So, this glossary includes the names of more than 70 different grape varieties along with brief descriptions of their characteristics. The varietal name on a label tells you more than anything else about what to expect of the wine.

Other items in this vocabulary include short summaries of the regions and appellations of recommended wines and some of the many label designations given to the style, alleged quality and regulatory classifications.

Finally, I have attempted to explain in simple and rational terms the many peculiar words I use in trying to convey the characteristics of wines described. 'Delicious' might need no further qualification, but the likes of 'bouncy', 'green' and 'liquorous' probably do.

A

abboccato – Medium-dry white wine style. Italy, especially Orvieto.

AC – See Appellation d'Origine Contrôlée.

acidity – To be any good, every wine must have the right level of acidity. It gives wine the element of dryness or sharpness it needs to prevent cloying sweetness or dull wateriness. If there is too much acidity, wine tastes raw or acetic (vinegary). Winemakers strive to create balanced acidity – either by cleverly controlling the natural processes, or by adding sugar and acid to correct imbalances.

aftertaste – The flavour that lingers in the mouth after swallowing the wine.

Aglianico – Black grape variety of southern Italy. It has romantic associations. When the ancient Greeks first colonised Italy in the seventh century BC, it was with the prime purpose of planting it as a vineyard (the Greek name for Italy was Oenotria – land of cultivated vines). The name for the vines the Greeks brought with them was Ellenico (as in Hellas, Greece), from which Aglianico is the modern rendering. To return to the point, these ancient vines, especially in the arid volcanic landscapes of Basilicata, produce excellent dark, earthy and highly distinctive wines. A name to look out for.

agriculture biologique – On French wine labels, an indication that the wine has been made by organic methods.

Albariño – White grape variety of Spain that makes intriguingly perfumed, fresh and spicy dry wines, especially in esteemed Rias Baixas region.

Almansa – DO winemaking region of Spain inland from Alicante, making great-value red wines.

alcohol – The alcohol levels in wines are expressed in terms of alcohol by volume ('abv'), that is, the percentage of the volume of the wine that is common, or ethyl, alcohol. A typical wine at 12% abv is thus 12 parts alcohol and, in effect, 88 parts fruit juice.

The question of how much alcohol we can drink without harming ourselves in the short or long term is an impossible one to answer, but there is more or less general agreement among scientists that small amounts of alcohol are good for us, even if the only evidence of this is actuarial – the fact that mortality statistics show teetotallers live significantly shorter lives than moderate drinkers. According to the Department of Health, there are 'safe limits' to the amount of alcohol we should drink weekly. These limits are measured in units of alcohol, with a small glass of wine taken to be one unit. Men are advised that 28 units a week is the most they can drink without risk to health, and for women (whose liver function differs from men's because of metabolic variations) the figure is 21 units.

If you wish to measure your consumption closely, note that a standard 75 cl bottle of wine at 12% alcohol contains nine units. A bottle of German Moselle at 8% alcohol has only six units, but a bottle of Australian Chardonnay at 14% has 10.5.

Alentejo – Wine region of southern Portugal (immediately north of the Algarve), with a fast-improving reputation, especially for sappy, keen reds from local grape varieties including Aragones, Castelão and Trincadeira grapes.

Alsace – France's easternmost wine-producing region lies between the Vosges Mountains and the River Rhine, with Germany beyond. These conditions make for the production of some of the world's most delicious and fascinating white wines, always sold under the name of their constituent grapes. Pinot Blanc is the most affordable – and is well worth looking out for. The 'noble' grape varieties of the region are Gewürztraminer, Muscat, Riesling and Tokay Pinot Gris, and they are always made on a single-variety basis. The richest, most exotic wines are those from individual grand cru vineyards, which are named on the label. Some vendange tardive (late harvest) wines are made, but tend to be expensive. All the wines are sold in tall, slim green bottles known as flûtes that closely resemble those of the Mosel, and the names of producers and grape varieties are often German too, so it is widely assumed that Alsace wines are German in style, if not in nationality. But this is not the case in either particular. Alsace wines are dry and quite unique in character – and definitely French.

Amarone – Style of red wine made in Valpolicella, Italy. Specially selected grapes are held back from the harvest and stored for several months to dry them out. They are then pressed and fermented into a highly concentrated speciality dry wine. Amarone means 'bitter', describing the dry style of the flavour.

amontillado – See Sherry.

aperitif – If a wine is thus described, I believe it will give more pleasure before a meal than with one. Crisp, low-alcohol German wines and other delicately flavoured whites (including many dry Italians) are examples.

Appellation d'Origine Contrôlée – Commonly abbreviated to AC or AOC, this is the system under which quality wines are defined in France. About a third of the country's vast annual output qualifies, and there are more than 400 distinct AC zones. The declaration of an AC on the label signifies that the wine meets standards concerning location of vineyards and wineries, grape varieties and limits on harvest per hectare, methods of cultivation and vinification, and alcohol content. Wines are inspected and tasted by state-appointed committees. The one major aspect of any given wine that an AC cannot guarantee is that you will like it – but it certainly improves the chances.

Apulia – Anglicised name for Puglia.

Ardèche – Region of southern France to the west of the Rhône valley, home to a good vin de pays zone known as the Coteaux de L'Ardèche. Lots of decent-value reds from Syrah grapes, and some, less-interesting, dry whites.

Assyrtiko – White grape variety of Greece now commonly named on dry white wines, sometimes of great quality, from the mainland and islands.

Asti – Town and major winemaking centre in Piedmont, Italy. The sparkling (spumante) sweet wines made from Moscato grapes are inexpensive and often delicious. Typical alcohol level is a modest 5 to 7%.

attack – In wine tasting, the first impression made by the wine in the mouth.

Auslese – German wine-quality designation. See QmP.

B

backbone – A personal item of wine-tasting terminology. It's the impression given by a well-made wine in which the flavours are a pleasure to savour at all three stages: initial sensation in the mouth; while being held in the mouth; in the aftertaste when the wine has been swallowed or spat out. Such a wine is held together by backbone.

Baga – Black grape variety indigenous to Portugal. Makes famously concentrated, juicy reds that get their deep colour from the grape's particularly thick skins. Look out for this name, now quite frequently quoted as the varietal on Portuguese wine labels. Often very good value for money.

balance – A big word in the vocabulary of wine tasting. Respectable wine must get two key things right: lots of fruitiness from the sweet grape juice, and plenty of acidity so the sweetness is 'balanced' with the crispness familiar in good dry whites and the dryness that marks out good reds. Some wines are noticeably 'well balanced' in that they have memorable fruitiness and the clean, satisfying 'finish' (last flavour in the mouth) that ideal acidity imparts.

Barbera – Black grape variety originally of Piedmont in Italy. Most commonly seen as Barbera d'Asti, the vigorously fruity red wine made around Asti – which is better known for sweet sparkling Asti Spumante. Barbera grapes are now being grown in South America, often producing a sleeker, smoother style than at home in Italy.

Bardolino – Once fashionable, light red wine DOC of Veneto, north-west Italy. Bardolino is made principally from Corvina Veronese grapes, plus Rondinella, Molinara and Negrara. Best wines are supposed to be those labelled classico, and superiore is applied to those aged a year and having at least 11.5% alcohol.

Barossa Valley – Famed vineyard region north of Adelaide, Australia, produces hearty reds principally from Shiraz, Cabernet Sauvignon and Grenache grapes, plus plenty of lush white wine from Chardonnay. Also known for limey, long-lived, mineral dry whites from Riesling grapes.

barrique – 'Barrel' in French. 'En barrique' on a wine label signifies the wine has been matured in oak.

Beaujolais – Unique red wines from the southern reaches of Burgundy, France, are made from Gamay grapes. Beaujolais nouveau, the new wine of each harvest, is released on the third Thursday of every November to much ballyhoo. It provides a friendly introduction to this deliciously bouncy, fleshily fruity wine style. Decent Beaujolais for enjoying during the rest of the year has lately become rather more expensive. If splashing out, go for Beaujolais Villages, from the region's better, northern vineyards. There are ten AC zones within the northern part of the region making wines under their own names. Known as 'the crus', these are Brouilly, Chénas, Chiroubles, Côte de Brouilly, Fleurie, Juliénas, Morgon, Moulin à Vent, Regnié and St Amour, and they produce most of the very best wines of the region – at prices a pound or two higher than for Beaujolais Villages.

Beaumes de Venise – Village near Châteauneuf du Pape in France's Rhône valley, famous for sweet and alcoholic wine from Muscat grapes. Delicious, grapey wines. A small number of growers also make strong (sometimes rather tough) red wines under the village name.

Beaune – One of the two winemaking centres (the other is Nuits St Georges) at the heart of Burgundy, in France. Three of the region's humbler appellations take the name of the town: Côtes de Beaune, Côtes de Beaune Villages and Hautes Côtes de Beaune. Wines made under these ACs are often, but by no means always, good value for money.

berry fruit – Some red wines deliver a burst of flavour in the mouth that corresponds to biting into a newly picked berry – strawberry, blackberry, etc. So a wine described as having berry fruit (by this writer, anyway) has freshness, liveliness, immediate appeal.

bianco – White wine, Italy.

Bical – White grape variety principally of Dão region of northern Portugal. Not usually identified on labels, because most of it goes into inexpensive sparkling wines. Can make still wines of very refreshing crispness.

biodynamics – A cultivation method taking the organic approach several steps further. Biodynamic winemakers plant and tend their vineyards according to a date and time calendar 'in harmony' with the movements of the planets. Some of France's best-known wine estates subscribe, and many more are going that way. It might all sound bonkers, but it's salutary to learn that biodynamics is based on principles first described by a very eminent man, the Austrian educationist Rudolph Steiner. He's lately been in the news for having written, in 1919, that farmers crazy enough to feed animal products to cattle would drive their livestock 'mad'.

bite – In wine tasting, the impression on the palate of a wine with plenty of acidity and, often, tannin.

blanc – White wine, France.

blanc de blancs – White wine from white grapes, France. May seem to be stating the obvious, but some white wines (e.g. champagne) are made, partially or entirely, from black grapes.

blanc de noirs – White wine from black grapes, France. Usually sparkling (especially champagne), made from black Pinot Meunier and Pinot Noir grapes, with no Chardonnay or other white varieties.

blanco – White wine, Spain and Portugal.

Blauer Zweigelt – Black grape variety of Austria, making a large proportion of the country's red wines, some of excellent quality.

Bobal – Black grape variety, mostly of south-eastern Spain. Thick skin is good for colour, and juice contributes acidity to blends.

bodega – In Spain, a wine producer or wine shop.

Bonarda – Black grape variety of northern Italy. Now more widely planted in Argentina, where it makes rather elegant red wines, often representing great value.

botrytis – Full name *botrytis cinerea*, is that of a beneficent fungus that can attack ripe grape bunches late in the season, shrivelling the berries to a gruesome-looking mess, which yields concentrated juice of prized sweetness. Cheerfully known as 'noble rot', this fungus is actively encouraged by winemakers in regions as diverse as Sauternes (in Bordeaux), Monbazillac (in Bergerac), the Rhine and Mosel valleys and South Australia to make ambrosial dessert wines.

bouncy – The feel in the mouth of a red wine with young, juicy fruitiness. Good Beaujolais is bouncy, as are many north-west Italian wines from Barbera and Dolcetto grapes.

Bourgogne Grand Ordinaire – Appellation of France's Burgundy region for 'ordinary' red wines from either Gamay or Pinot Noir grapes, or both.

Bourgueil – Appellation of Loire Valley, France. Long-lived red wines from Cabernet Franc grapes.

briary – In wine-tasting, associated with the flavours of fruit from prickly bushes such as blackberries.

brûlé – Pleasant burnt-toffee taste or smell, as in crème brûlée.

brut – Driest style of sparkling wine. Originally French, for very dry champagnes specially developed for the British market, but now used for sparkling wines from all round the world.

Buzet – Little-seen AC of south-west France overshadowed by Bordeaux but producing some characterful ripe reds.

C

Cabardès – New AC (1998) for red and rosé wines from area north of Carcassonne, Aude, France. Principally Cabernet Sauvignon and Merlot grapes.

Cabernet franc – Black grape variety originally of France. It makes the light-bodied and keenly edged red wines of the Loire Valley – such as Chinon and Saumur. And it is much grown in Bordeaux, especially in the appellation of St Emilion. Also now planted in Argentina, Australia and North America. The wines, especially in the Loire, are characterised by a leafy, sappy style and bold fruitiness. Most are best enjoyed young.

Cabernet Sauvignon – Black (or, rather, blue) grape variety now grown in virtually every wine-producing nation. When perfectly ripened, the grapes are smaller than many other varieties and have particularly thick skins. This means that when pressed Cabernet grapes have a high proportion of skin to juice – and that makes for wine with lots of colour and tannin. In Bordeaux, the grape's traditional home, the grandest Cabernet-based wines have always been known as vins de garde (wines to keep) because they take years – even decades – to evolve, as the effect of all that skin extraction preserves the fruit all the way to magnificent maturity. But in today's impatient world, these grapes are exploited in modern winemaking techniques to produce the sublime flavours of mature Cabernet without having to hang around for lengthy periods awaiting maturation. While there's nothing like a fine, ten-year-old claret (and nothing quite as expensive), there are many excellent Cabernets from around the world that amply illustrate this grape's characteristics. Classic smells and flavours include blackcurrants, cedar wood, chocolate, tobacco – even violets.

Cahors – An AC of the Lot Valley in south-west France once famous for 'black wine'. This was a curious concoction of straightforward wine mixed with a soupy must, made by boiling up new-pressed juice to concentrate it (through evaporation) before fermentation. The myth is still perpetuated that Cahors wine continues to be made in this way, but production on this basis actually ceased 150 years ago. Cahors today is no stronger, or blacker, than the wines of neighbouring appellations.

Cairanne – Village of the appellation collectively known as the Côtes du Rhône Villages in south France. Cairanne is one of several villages entitled to put their name on the labels of wines made within their AC boundary, and the appearance of this name is quite reliably an indicator of a very good wine indeed.

Calatayud – DO (quality wine zone) near Zaragoza in the Aragon region of northern Spain where they're making some astonishingly good wines at bargain prices, mainly reds from Garnacha and Tempranillo grapes. These are the varieties that go into the light and oaky wines of Rioja, but in Calatayud, the wines are dark, dense and decidedly different.

cantina sociale – See Co-op.

Carignan – Black grape variety of Mediterranean France. It is rarely identified on labels, but is a major constituent of wines from the southern Rhône and Languedoc-Roussillon regions, especially the cheaper brands. Known as Carignano in Italy and Cariñena in Spain.

Carmenère – Black grape variety once widely grown in Bordeaux but abandoned due to cultivation problems. Lately revived in South America, where it is producing fine wines.

cassis – As a tasting note, signifies that a wine has a noticeable blackcurrant-concentrate flavour or smell. Much associated with the Cabernet Sauvignon grape.

Castelao – Portuguese black grape variety. Same as Periquita.

Catarratto – White grape variety of Sicily. In skilled hands it can make anything from keen, green-fruit dry whites to lush, oaked super-ripe styles. Also used for marsala.

cat's pee – In tasting notes, a mildly jocular reference to the smell of a certain style of Sauvignon Blanc wine.

cava – The sparkling wine of Spain. Most originates in Catalonia, but the Denominacion de Origen (DO) guarantee of authenticity is open to producers in many regions of the country. Much cava is very reasonably priced even though it is made by the same method as champagne – second fermentation in bottle, known in Spain as the 'metodo classico'.

CdR – Côtes du Rhône.

Cépage – Grape variety, French. 'Cépage Merlot' on a label simply means the wine is made largely or exclusively from Merlot grapes.

Chablis – Northernmost AC of France's Burgundy region. Its dry white wines from Chardonnay grapes are known for their fresh and steely style, but the best wines also age very gracefully into complex classics.

Chambourcin – Sounds like a cream cheese but it's a relatively modern (1963) French hybrid black grape that makes some good non-appellation lightweight-but-concentrated reds in the Loire Valley and now some heftier versions in Australia.

Chardonnay – The world's most popular grape variety. Said to originate from the village of Chardonnay in the Mâconnais region of southern Burgundy, the vine is now planted in every wine-producing nation. Wines are commonly characterised by generous colour and sweet-apple smell, but styles range from lean and sharp to opulently rich. Australia started the craze for oaked Chardonnay, the gold-coloured, super-ripe, buttery, 'upfront' wines that are a caricature of lavish and outrageously expensive burgundies such as Meursault and Puligny-Montrachet. Rich to the point of egginess, these Aussie pretenders are now giving way to a sleeker, more minerally style with much less oak presence – if any at all. California and Chile, New Zealand and South Africa are competing hard to imitate the burgundian style, and Australia's success in doing so.

Châteauneuf du Pape – Famed appellation centred on a picturesque village of the southern Rhône valley in France where in the 1320s French Pope Clement V had a splendid new château built for himself as a country retreat amidst his vineyards. The red wines of the AC, which can be made from 13 different grape varieties but are principally from Grenache, Syrah and Mourvèdre, are regarded as the best of the southern Rhône and have become rather expensive – but they can be sensationally good. Expensive white wines are also made.

Chenin blanc – White grape variety of the Loire Valley, France. Now also grown farther afield, especially in South Africa. Makes dry, soft white wines and also rich, sweet styles. Sadly, many low-cost Chenin wines are bland and uninteresting.

cherry – In wine-tasting, either a pale red colour or, more commonly, a smell or flavour akin to the sun-warmed, bursting sweet ripeness of cherries. Many Italian wines, from lightweights such as Bardolino and Valpolicella to serious Chianti, have this character. 'Black cherry' as a description is often used of Merlot wines – meaning they are sweet but have a firmness associated with the thicker skins of black cherries.

Cinsault – Black grape variety of southern France, where it is invariably blended with others in wines of all qualities ranging from vin de pays to the pricy reds of Châteauneuf du Pape. Also much planted in South Africa. The effect in wine is to add keen aromas (sometimes compared with turpentine!) and softness to the blend. The name is often spelt Cinsaut.

Clape, La – A small cru (defined quality-vineyard area) within the Coteaux du Languedoc where the growers make some seriously delicious red wines, mainly from Carignan, Grenache and Syrah grapes. A name worth looking out for on labels from the region.

claret – The red wine of Bordeaux, France. It comes from Latin *clarus*, meaning 'clear', recalling a time when the red wines of the region were much lighter in colour than they are now.

clarete – On Spanish labels indicates a pale-coloured red wine. *Tinto* signifies a deeper hue.

classed growth – English translation of French *cru classé* describes a group of 60 individual wine estates in the Médoc district of Bordeaux, which in 1855 were granted this new status on the basis that their wines were the most expensive at that time. The classification was a promotional wheeze to attract attention to the Bordeaux stand at that year's Great Exhibition in Paris. Amazingly, all of the 60 wines concerned are still in production and most still occupy more or less their original places in the pecking order price-wise. The league was divided up into five divisions from Premier Grand Cru Classé (just four wines originally, with one promoted in 1971 – the only change ever made to the classification) to Cinquième Grand Cru Classé. Other regions of Bordeaux, notably Graves and St Emilion, have since imitated Médoc and introduced their own rankings of cru classé estates.

classic – An overused term in every respect – wine descriptions being no exception. In this book, the word is used to describe a very good wine of its type. So, a 'classic' Cabernet Sauvignon is one that is recognisably and admirably characteristic of that grape.

Classico – Under Italy's wine laws, this word appended to the name of a DOC zone has great significance. The classico wines of the region can only be made from vineyards lying in the best-rated areas, and wines thus labelled (for example Chianti Classico, Soave Classico, Valpolicella Classico) can be reliably counted on to be a cut above the rest.

Colombard – White grape variety of southern France. Once employed almost entirely for making the wine that is distilled for armagnac and cognac brandies, but lately restored to varietal prominence in the Vin de Pays des Côtes de Gascogne, where high-tech wineries turn it into a fresh and crisp, if unchallenging, dry wine at a budget price. But beware, cheap Colombard (especially from South Africa) can still be very dull.

Conca de Barbera – Winemaking region of Catalonia, Spain.

co-op – Very many of France's good-quality, inexpensive wines are made by co-operatives. These are wine-producing factories whose members, and joint-owners, are local vignerons (vine-growers). Each year they sell their harvests to the co-op for turning into branded wines. In Italy, co-op wines can be identified by the words 'Cantina Sociale' on the label and in Germany by the term 'Winzergenossenschaft'.

Corbières – A name to look out for. It's an AC of France's Midi (deep south) and produces countless robust reds and a few interesting whites, often at bargain prices.

Cortese – White grape variety of Piedmont, Italy. At its best, makes amazingly delicious, keenly brisk and fascinating wines, including those of the Gavi DOCG. Worth seeking out.

Costières de Nîmes – Until 1989, this AC of southern France was known as the Costières de Gard. It forms a buffer between the southern Rhône and Languedoc-Roussillon regions, and makes wines from broadly the same range of grape varieties. It's a name to look out for, the best red wines being notable for their concentration of colour and fruit, with the earthy-spiciness of the better Rhône wines and a likeable liquorice note. A few good white wines, too, and even a decent rosé or two.

Côte – In French, it simply means a side, or slope, of a hill. The implication in wine terms is that the grapes come from a vineyard ideally situated for maximum sunlight, good drainage and the unique soil conditions prevailing on the hill in question. It's fair enough to claim that vines grown on slopes might get more sunlight than those grown on the flat, but there is no guarantee whatsoever that any wine labelled 'Côtes du' this or that is made from grapes grown on a hillside. Côtes du Rhône wines are a case in point. Many 'Côtes' wines come from entirely level vineyards, and it is worth remembering that many of the vineyards of Bordeaux, producing most of the world's priciest wines, are little short of prairie-flat. The quality factor is determined much more significantly by the weather and the talents of the winemaker.

Côtes de Blaye - Appellation Contrôlée zone of Bordeaux on the right bank of the River Gironde, opposite the more prestigious Médoc zone of the left bank. A couple of centuries ago, Blaye (pronounced 'bligh') was the grander of the two, and even today makes some wines that compete well for quality, and at a fraction of the price of wines from its more fashionable rival across the water.

Côtes du Luberon – Appellation Contrôlée zone of Provence in south-east France. Wines, mostly red, are similar in style to Côtes du Rhône.

Côtes du Rhône – One of the biggest and best-known appellations of south-east France, covering an area roughly defined by the southern reaches of the valley of the River Rhône. Long notorious for cheap and execrable reds, the Côtes du Rhône AC has lately achieved remarkable improvements in quality at all points along the price scale. Lots of brilliant-value warm and spicy reds, principally from Grenache and Syrah grapes. There are also some white and rosé wines. Note that this region had a brilliant run of vintages up to 2001 but then a rain-and-storm-ruined one in 2002 and an overheated one in 2003. Go for pre-2002 vintages if you have a choice.

Côtes du Rhône Villages – Appellation within the larger Côtes du Rhône AC for wine of supposed superiority made in a number of zones associated with a long list of nominated individual villages. Village wines may be more interesting than their humbler counterparts, but don't count on it.

Côtes du Roussillon – Huge appellation of south-west France known for strong, dark, peppery reds often offering very decent value.

Côtes du Roussillon Villages – Appellation for superior wines from a number of nominated locations within the larger Roussillon AC. Some of these village wines can be of exceptional quality and value.

crianza – Means 'nursery' in Spanish. On Rioja and Navarra wines, the designation signifies a wine that has been nursed through a maturing period of at least a year in oak casks and a further six months in bottle before being released for sale.

cru – A word that crops up with confusing regularity on French wine labels. It means 'the growing' or 'the making' of a wine and asserts that the wine concerned is from a specific vineyard. Under the Appellation Contrôlée rules, countless crus are classified in various hierarchical ranks. Hundreds of individual vineyards are described as premier cru or grand cru in the classic wine regions of Alsace, Bordeaux, Burgundy and Champagne. The common denominator is that the wine can be counted on to be expensive. On humbler wines, the use of the word cru tends to be mere decoration.

cru classé – See Classed growth.

cuve – A vat for wine, French.

cuvée – French for the wine in a cuve, or vat. The word is much used on labels to imply that the wine is from just one vat, and thus of unique, unblended character. Premier cuvée is supposedly the best wine from a given pressing because the grapes have had only the initial, gentle squashing to extract the free-run juice. Subsequent cuvées will have been from harsher pressings, grinding the grape pulp to extract the last drop of juice.

D

Dão – Major wine-producing region of northern Portugal now turning out much more interesting reds than it used to – worth looking out for anything made by mega-producer Sogrape.

demi sec – 'Half-dry' style of French (and some other) wines. Beware. It can mean anything from off-dry to cloyingly sweet.

DO – Denominacion de Origen, Spain's wine-regulating scheme, similar to France's AC but older – the first DO region was Rioja, from 1926. DO wines are Spain's best, accounting for a third of the nation's annual production.

DOC – Stands for Denominazione di Origine Controllata, Italy's equivalent of France's AC. The wines are made according to the stipulations of each of its 280 denominated zones of origin, 20 of which enjoy the superior classification of DOCG (DOC with *e Garantita* – 'guaranteed' – appended).

Durif – Rare black grape variety mostly of California, where it is also known as Petite Sirah, but with some plantings in Australia.

E

earthy – A tricky word in the wine vocabulary. In this book, its use is meant to be complimentary. It indicates that the wine somehow suggests the soil the grapes were grown in, even (perhaps a shade too poetically) the landscape in which the vineyards lie. The amazing-value red wines of the torrid, volcanic southernmost regions of Italy are often described as earthy. This is an association with the pleasantly 'scorched' back-flavour in wines made from the ultra-ripe harvests of this near-sub-tropical part of the world.

edge – A wine with edge is one with evident (although not excessive) acidity.

élevé – 'Brought up' in French. Much used on wine labels where the wine has been matured (brought up) in oak barrels *'élevé en fûts de chêne'* to give it extra dimensions.

Entre Deux Mers – Meaning 'between two seas', it's a region lying between the Dordogne and Garonne rivers of Bordeaux, now mainly known for dry white wines from Sauvignon and Semillon grapes. Quality rarely seems exciting.

Estremadura – Wine-producing region occupying Portugal's coastal area north of Lisbon. Lots of interesting wines from indigenous grape varieties, usually at bargain prices. If a label mentions Estremadura, it is a safe rule that there may be something good within.

F

Faugères – AC of the Languedoc in south-west France. Source of many hearty, economic reds.

Feteasca – White grape variety widely grown in Romania. Name means 'maiden's grape' and the wine tends to be soft and slightly sweet.

Fiano – White grape variety of Sicily, lately revived. It is said to have been cultivated by the ancient Romans for a wine called Apianum.

finish – The last flavour lingering in the mouth after wine has been swallowed.

fino – Pale and very dry style of sherry. You drink it thoroughly chilled – and you don't keep it any longer after opening than other dry white wines. Needs to be fresh to be at its best.

Fitou – One of the first 'designer' wines, it's an appellation in France's Languedoc region, where production is dominated by one huge co-operative, the Vignerons de Mont Tauch. Back in the 1970s, this co-op paid a corporate-image company to come up with a Fitou logo and label-design style, and the wines have prospered ever since. And it's not just packaging – Fitou at all price levels can be very good value, especially from the Mont Tauch co-op.

flabby – Fun word describing a wine that tastes dilute or watery, with insufficient acidity.

flying winemaker – Back-labels on supermarket wines used to boast that the contents were made by a flying winemaker. Less is made of this feature of international winemaking now, although these consultants are as numerous as ever. They visit vineyards worldwide at harvest time to oversee the production process, perhaps to ensure that the style of wine wanted by a major customer (usually a supermarket) is adhered to by the locals. Flying winemakers are very often Australian, with degrees in oenology (the science of winemaking) and well up on the latest technology and biochemistry. If there is a criticism of them, it is that they have a tendency to impose a uniform style on all the vineyards upon which they descend.

fruit – In tasting terms, the fruit is the greater part of the overall flavour of a wine. The wine is (or should be) after all, composed entirely of fruit.

G

Gamay – The black grape that makes all red Beaujolais. It is a pretty safe rule to avoid Gamay wines from any other region. It's a grape that does not do well elsewhere.

Garganega – White grape variety of the Veneto region of north-east Italy. Best known as the principal ingredient of Soave, but occasionally included in varietal blends and mentioned as such on labels. Correctly pronounced 'gar-GAN-iga'.

Garnacha – Spanish black grape variety synonymous with Grenache of France. It is blended with Tempranillo to make the red wines of Rioja and Navarra, and is now quite widely cultivated elsewhere in Spain to make grippingly fruity varietals.

garrigue – Arid land of France's deep south giving its name to a style of red wine that notionally evokes the herby, heated, peppery flavours associated with such a landscape. A tricky metaphor!

Gavi – DOCG for dry but rich white wine from Cortese grapes in Piedmont, north-west Italy. Trendy Gavi di Gavi wines tend to be enjoyably lush, but are rather expensive.

Gewürztraminer – One of the great grape varieties of Alsace, France. At their best, the wines are perfumed with lychees and are richly, spicily fruity, yet quite dry. Gewürztraminer from Alsace is almost always expensive, but the grape is also grown with some success in Eastern Europe, Germany, Italy and South America, and sold at more approachable prices. Pronounced 'geh-VOORTS-traminner'.

Graciano – Black grape variety of Spain that is one of the minor constituents of Rioja. Better known in its own right in Australia, where it can make dense, spicy, long-lived red wines.

green – In flavour, a wine that is unripe and raw-tasting.

Grenache – The mainstay of the wines of the southern Rhône Valley in France. Grenache is usually the greater part of the mix in Côtes du Rhône reds and is widely planted right across the neighbouring Languedoc-Roussillon region. It's a big-cropping variety that thrives even in the hottest climates and is really a blending grape – most commonly with Syrah, the noble variety of the northern Rhône. Few French wines are labelled with its name, but the grape has caught on in Australia in a big way and it is now becoming a familiar varietal, known for strong, dark liquorous reds. Grenache is the French name for what is originally a Spanish variety, Garnacha.

Grillo – White grape of Sicily said to be among the island's oldest indigenous varieties, pre-dating the arrival of the Greeks in 600BC. Much used for fortified marsala, it has lately been revived for interesting, aromatic dry table wines.

grip – In wine-tasting terminology, the sensation in the mouth produced by a wine that has a healthy quantity of tannin in it. A wine with grip is a good wine. A wine with too much tannin, or which is still too young (the tannin hasn't 'softened' with age), is not described as having grip but as mouth-puckering – or simply undrinkable.

Grüner Veltliner – The 'national' white-wine grape of Austria. In the past it made mostly soft, German-style everyday wines, but now is behind some excellent dry styles, too.

H

halbtrocken – 'Half-dry' in Germany's wine vocabulary. A reassurance that the wine is not some ghastly sugared Liebfraumilch-style confection.

hock – The wine of Germany's Rhine river valleys. It comes in brown bottles, as distinct from the wine of the Mosel river valleys – which comes in green ones.

I

Indicazione Geografica Tipica – Italy's recently instituted wine-quality designation, broadly equivalent to France's vin de pays. The label has to state the geographical location of the vineyard and will often (but not always) state the principal grape varieties from which the wine is made.

Inycon – A recent wine brand of Sicily's huge Settesoli co-operative and the label on several wines mentioned in this book. Inycon was the Ancient Greek name of the modern Sicilian village of Menfi, where the vineyards and winery for the brand have been established.

J

jammy – the 'sweetness' in dry red wines is supposed to evoke ripeness rather than sugariness. Sometimes, flavours include a sweetness reminiscent of jam. Usually a fault in the winemaking technique.

joven – Young wine, Spanish. In regions such as Rioja, vino joven is a synonym for *sin crianza*, which means 'without ageing' in cask or bottle.

K

Kabinett – Under Germany's bewildering wine-quality rules, this is a classification of a top-quality (QmP) wine. Expect a keen, dry, racy style. The name comes from the cabinet or cupboard in which winemakers traditionally kept their most treasured bottles.

Kekfrankos – Black grape variety of Hungary, particularly the Sopron region, which makes some of the country's more interesting red wines, characterised by colour and spiciness. Same variety as Austria's Blaufrankisch.

L

Lambrusco – The name is that of a black grape variety widely grown across northern Italy. True Lambrusco wine is red, dry and slightly sparkling, but from the 1980s Britain has been deluged with a strange, sweet manifestation of the style, which has done little to enhance the good name of the original. Good Lambrusco is delicious and fun.

Languedoc-Roussillon – Vast area of southern France, including the country's south-west Mediterranean region. The source, now, of many great-value wines from countless ACs and vin de pays zones.

legs – The colourless residue left clinging to the sides of the glass after wine has been swirled. The persistence of the legs is an indicator of the weight of alcohol. Also known as 'tears'.

lieu dit – This is starting to appear on French wine labels. It translates as 'agreed place' and is an area of vineyard defined as of particular character or merit but not classified under wine law. Usually, the lieu dit's name is stated, with the implication that the wine in question has special value.

liquorice – The pungent, slightly burnt flavours of this once-fashionable confection are detectable in some wines made from very ripe grapes, for example, the Malbec harvested in Argentina and several varieties grown in the very hot vineyards of southernmost Italy. A close synonym is 'tarry'. This characteristic is by no means a fault in red wine, unless very dominant, but it can make for a challenging flavour that might not appeal to all tastes.

liquorous – Wines of great weight and glyceriney texture (evidenced by the 'legs', or 'tears', which cling to the glass after the wine has been swirled) are always noteworthy. The connection with liquor is drawn in respect of the feel of the wine in the mouth, rather than with the higher alcoholic strength of spirits.

Lugana – DOC of Lombardy, Italy, known for a dry white wine that is often of real distinction – rich, almondy stuff from the ubiquitous Trebbiano grape.

M

Macabeo – One of the main grapes used for cava, the sparkling wine of Spain. It is the same grape as Viura.

Mâcon – Town and collective appellation of southern Burgundy, France. Lightweight white wines from Chardonnay grapes and similarly light reds from Pinot Noir and some Gamay. The better ones, and the ones exported, have the AC Mâcon-Villages and there are individual-village wines with their own ACs including Mâcon-Clessé, Mâcon-Viré and Mâcon-Lugny.

Malbec – Black grape variety grown on a small scale in Bordeaux, and the mainstay of the wines of Cahors in France's Dordogne region under the name Cot. Now much better known for producing big butch reds in Argentina.

Mantinia – Winemaking region of the Peloponnese, Greece. Dry whites from Moschofilero grapes are aromatic and refreshing.

Manzanilla – Pale, very dry sherry of Sanlucar de Barrameda, a delightful seaport on the southernmost coast of Spain. Manzanilla is proud to be distinct from the pale, very dry fino sherry of the main producing town of Jerez de la Frontera down the coast. Drink it chilled and fresh – it goes downhill in an opened bottle after just a few days, even if kept (as it should be) in the fridge.

Margaret River – Vineyard region of Western Australia regarded as ideal for grape varieties including Cabernet Sauvignon. It has a relatively cool climate and a reputation for making sophisticated wines, both red and white.

Marlborough – Best-known vineyard region of New Zealand's South Island has a cool climate and a name for brisk but cerebral Sauvignon Blanc and Chardonnay wines.

Marsanne – White grape variety of the northern Rhône Valley and, increasingly, of the wider south of France. It's known for making well coloured wines with heady aroma and fruit.

Mataro – Black grape variety of Australia. It's the same as the Mourvèdre of France and Monastrell of Spain.

McLaren Vale – Vineyard region south of Adelaide in south-east Australia. Known for serious-quality wines from grape varieties including Shiraz and Chardonnay.

meaty – Weighty, rich red wine style.

Mendoza – The region to watch in Argentina. Lying to the east of the Andes mountains, just about opposite the best vineyards of Chile on the other side, Mendoza accounts for the bulk of Argentine wine production, with quality improving fast.

Merlot – One of the great black wine grapes of Bordeaux, and now grown all over the world. The name is said to derive from the French *merle*, meaning a blackbird. Characteristics of Merlot-based wines attract descriptions such as 'plummy' and 'plump' with black-cherry aroma. The grapes are larger than most, and thus have less skin in proportion to their flesh. This means the resulting wines have less tannin than wines from smaller-berry varieties such as Cabernet Sauvignon, and are therefore, in the Bordeaux context at least, more suitable for drinking while still relatively young.

Midi – Catch-all term for the deep south of France, west of the Rhône Valley.

mineral – Good dry white wines can have a crispness and freshness that somehow evokes this word. Purity of flavour is a key.

Minervois – AC for (mostly) red wines from vineyards around the town of Minerve in the Languedoc-Roussillon region of France. Often good value. The new Minervois La Livinière AC – a sort of Minervois Grand Cru – is host to some great estates, including Château Maris and Vignobles Lorgeril.

Monastrell – Black grape variety of Spain, widely planted in Mediterranean regions for inexpensive wines notable for their high alcohol and toughness – though they can mature into excellent, soft reds. The variety is known in France as Mourvèdre and in Australia as Mataro.

Monbazillac – AC for sweet, dessert wines within the wider appellation of Bergerac in south-west France. Made from the same grape varieties (principally Sauvignon and Semillon) that go into the much costlier counterpart wines of Barsac and Sauternes in Bordeaux, these stickies from botrytis-affected, late-harvested grapes can be delicious and good value for money.

Montalcino – Hill town of Tuscany, Italy, and a DOCG for strong and very long-lived red wines from Brunello grapes. The wines are mostly very expensive. Rosso di Montalcino, a DOC for the humbler wines of the zone, is often a good buy.

Montepulciano – Black grape variety of Italy. Best-known in Montepulciano d'Abruzzo, the juicy, purply-black and bramble-fruited red of the Abruzzi region mid-way down Italy's Adriatic side. Also the grape in the rightly popular hearty reds of Rosso Conero from around Ancona in the Marches. Not to be confused with the hill town of

Montepulciano in Tuscany, famous for expensive Vino Nobile di Montepulciano wine.

morello – Lots of red wines have smells and flavours redolent of cherries. Morello cherries, among the darkest-coloured and sweetest of all varieties and the preferred choice of cherry brandy producers, have a distinct sweetness resembled by some wines made from Merlot grapes. A morello whiff or taste is generally very welcome.

Moscatel – Spanish Muscat.

Moscato – See Muscat.

Moselle – The wine of Germany's Mosel river valleys, collectively known for winemaking purposes as Mosel-Saar-Ruwer. The wine always comes in slim, green bottles, as distinct from the brown bottles employed for Rhine wines.

Mourvèdre – Widely planted black grape variety of southern France. It's an ingredient in many of the wines of Provence, the Rhône and Languedoc, including the ubiquitous Vin de Pays d'Oc. It's a hot climate vine and the wine is usually blended with other varieties to give sweet aromas and 'backbone' to the mix. Known as Mataro in Australia and Monastrell in Spain.

Muscadet – One of France's most familiar everyday whites. It comes from vineyards at the estuarial end of the river Loire, and at its best has something of a sea-breezy freshness about it. The better wines are reckoned to be those from the vineyards in the Sèvre et Maine region, and many are made *sur lie* – 'on the lees' – meaning that the wine is left in contact with the yeasty deposit of its fermentation until just before bottling, in an endeavour to add interest to what can sometimes be an acidic and fruitless style.

Muscat – Grape variety with origins in ancient Greece, and still grown widely in the Aegean islands for the production of sweet white wines. Muscats are the wines that taste more like grape-juice than any other – but the high sugar levels ensure they are also among the most alcoholic of wines, too. Known as Moscato in Italy, the grape is much used for making sweet sparkling wines, as in Asti Spumante or Moscato d'Asti. There are several appellations in south-west France for inexpensive Muscats made rather like port, part-fermented before the addition of grape alcohol to halt the conversion of sugar into alcohol, creating a sweet and heady *vin doux naturel*. Dry Muscat wines, when well made, have a delicious sweet aroma but a refreshing, light touch with flavours reminiscent variously of orange blossom, wood smoke and grapefruit.

must – New-pressed grape juice prior to fermentation.

N

Navarra – DO wine-producing region of northern Spain adjacent to, and overshadowed by, Rioja. Navarra's wines can be startlingly akin to their neighbouring rivals, and sometimes rather better value for money.

négociant – In France, a dealer-producer who buys wines from growers and matures and/or blends them for sale under his own label. Purists can be a bit sniffy about these entrepreneurs, claiming that only the vine-grower with his or her own winemaking set-up can make truly authentic stuff, but the truth is that many of the best wines of France are négociant-produced – especially at the humbler end of the price scale. Négociants are often identified on wine labels as négociant-éleveur (literally 'dealer-bringer-up'), meaning that the wine has been matured, blended and bottled by the party in question.

Negro Amaro – Black grape variety mainly of Apulia, the fast-improving wine region of south-east Italy. Dense, earthy red wines with ageing potential and plenty of alcohol. The grape behind Copertino.

Nero d'Avola – Black grape variety of Sicily and southern Italy. It makes deep-coloured wines that, given half a chance, can develop intensity and richness with age.

non-vintage – A wine is described as such when it has been blended from the harvests of more than one year. A non-vintage wine is not necessarily an inferior one, but under quality control regulations around the world, still table wines must usually derive solely from one year's grape crop to qualify for appellation status. Champagnes and sparkling wines are mostly blended from several vintages, as are fortified wines, such as sherry and basic port.

nose – In the vocabulary of the wine-taster, the nose is the scent of a wine. Sounds a bit dotty, but it makes a sensible-enough alternative to the rather bald 'smell'. The use of the word 'perfume' implies that the wine smells particularly good. 'Aroma' is used specifically to describe a wine that smells as it should, as in 'this Burgundy has the authentic strawberry-raspberry aroma of Pinot Noir'.

O

oak – Most of the world's more expensive wines are matured in new or nearly new oak barrels, giving additional opulence of flavour. Of late, many cheaper wines have been getting the oak treatment, too, in older, cheaper casks, or simply by having sacks of oak chippings poured into their steel or fibreglass holding tanks. 'Oak aged' on a label is likely to indicate the latter treatments. But the overtly oaked wines of Australia have in some cases been so overdone that there is now a reactive trend whereby some producers proclaim their wines – particularly Chardonnays – as 'unoaked' on the label, thereby asserting that the flavours are more naturally achieved.

Oltrepo Pavese – Wine-producing zone of Piedmont, north-west Italy. The name means 'south of Pavia across the [river] Po', and the wines, both white and red, can be excellent quality and value for money.

organic wine – As in other sectors of the food industry, demand for organically made wine is – or appears to be – growing. As a rule, a wine qualifies as organic if it comes entirely from grapes grown in vineyards cultivated without the use of synthetic materials, and is made in a winery where chemical treatments or additives are shunned with similar vigour. In fact, there are plenty of winemakers in the world using organic methods but who disdain to label their bottles as such. Wines that do brazenly proclaim their organic status tend to carry the same sort of premium as their counterparts round the corner in the fruit, vegetable and meat aisles. The upshot is that there is only a limited choice of organic wine. There is no single worldwide (or even Europe-wide) standard for organic food or wine, so you pretty much have to take the producer's word for it.

P

Pasqua – One of the biggest and, it should be said, best wine producers of the Veneto region of north-east Italy.

Passetoutgrains – Bourgogne passetoutgrains is a generic appellation of the Burgundy region, France. The word loosely means 'any grapes allowed' and is supposed specifically to designate a red wine made with Gamay grapes as well as Burgundy's principal black variety, Pinot Noir, in a ratio of two parts Gamay to one of Pinot. The wine is usually relatively inexpensive, and relatively uninteresting, too.

Periquita – Black grape variety of southern Portugal. Makes rather exotic spicy reds. Name means 'parrot'.

Petite Sirah – Black grape variety of California and Latin America known for plenty of colour and long life. Not related to the Syrah of the Rhône.

Petit Verdot – Black grape variety of Bordeaux used to give additional colour, density and spiciness to Cabernet Sauvignon-dominated blends. Strictly a minority player at home, but in Australia and California it is grown as the principal variety for some big hearty reds of real character.

petrol – When white wines from certain grapes, especially Riesling, are allowed to age in the bottle for longer than a year or two, they can take on a spirity aroma reminiscent of petrol or diesel. In grand mature German wines, this is considered a very good thing.

Picpoul – Obscure grape variety of southern France. Best known in Picpoul de Pinet, a weighty-ish dry white from near Carcassonne in the Languedoc. The name Picpoul means 'stings the lips' – referring to the natural high acidity of the juice.

Piemonte – North-western province of Italy, which we call Piedmont, known for the spumante wines of the town of Asti, plus expensive Barbaresco and Barolo and better-value varietal red wines from Barbera and Dolcetto grapes.

Pinotage – South Africa's own black grape variety. Makes red wines ranging from light and juicy to dark, strong and long-lived. It's a cross between Pinot Noir and a grape the South Africans used to call Hermitage (thus the portmanteau name) but turns out to have been Cinsault. Cheaper Pinotages tend to disappoint, but there has been an improvement of late in the standard.

Pinot Blanc – White grape variety principally of Alsace, France. Florally perfumed, exotically fruity dry white wines.

Pinot Grigio – White grape variety of northern Italy. Wines bearing its name have become fashionable in recent times. Good examples have an interesting, smoky-pungent aroma and keen, slaking fruit. But most are dull. Originally a French grape, where it is known as Pinot Gris, it is renowned for making lushly exotic – and expensive – white wines in the Alsace region.

Pinot Noir – The great black grape of Burgundy, France. It makes all the region's great red wines. Notoriously difficult to grow in warmer climates, it is nevertheless cultivated by countless intrepid winemakers in the New World intent on reproducing the magic appeal of red Burgundy. California and New Zealand have come closest, but rarely at prices much below those for the real thing. Some Chilean Pinot Noirs (Cono Sur, for example) are inexpensive and of exciting quality.

Pouilly Fuissé – Village and AC of the Mâconnais region of southern Burgundy in France. Dry white wines from Chardonnay grapes. Wines are among the highest-rated of the Mâconnais.

Pouilly Fumé – Village and AC of the Loire Valley in France. Dry white wines from Sauvignon Blanc grapes. Similar 'pebbly', 'grassy' or even 'gooseberry' style to neighbouring AC Sancerre. The notion put about by some enthusiasts that Pouilly Fumé is 'smoky' is surely nothing more than word-association with the name.

Primitivo – Black grape variety of southern Italy, especially the region of Apulia/Puglia. The wines are typically dense and dark in colour with plenty of alcohol, and have an earthy, spicy style. Often a real bargain. It is believed to be closely related to California's Zinfandel, which makes purple, brambly wines of a very different hue.

Prosecco – White grape variety of Italy's Veneto region which gives its name to a light, sparkling and cheap wine that is much appreciated locally but not widely exported.

Puglia – The region occupying the 'heel' of southern Italy, and one of the world's fastest-improving sources of inexpensive wines. Modern winemaking techniques and large regional grants from the EU are largely responsible.

Q

QbA – German, standing for *Qualitätswein bestimmter Anbaugebiet*. It means 'quality wine from designated areas' and implies that the wine is made from grapes with a minimum level of ripeness, but it's by no means a guarantee of exciting quality. Only wines labelled QmP (see next entry) can be depended upon to be special.

QmP – Stands for *Qualitätswein mit Prädikat*. These are the serious wines of Germany, made without the addition of sugar to 'improve' them. To qualify for QmP status, the grapes must reach a level of ripeness as measured on a sweetness scale – all according to Germany's fiendishly complicated wine quality regulations. Wines from grapes that reach the stated minimum level of sweetness qualify for the description of Kabinett. The next level up earns the rank of Spätlese, meaning 'late-picked'. Kabinett wines can be expected to be dry and brisk in style, and Spätlese wines a little bit riper and fuller. The next grade up, Auslese, meaning 'selected harvest', indicates a wine made from super-ripe grapes; it will be golden in colour and honeyed in flavour. A generation ago, these wines were as valued, and as expensive, as any of the world's grandest appellations, but the collapse in demand for German wines in the UK – brought about by the disrepute rightly earned for floods of filthy Liebfraumilch – means they are now seriously undervalued.

Quincy – AC of Loire Valley, France, known for pebbly-dry white wines from Sauvignon grapes. The wines are forever compared to those of nearby and much better-known Sancerre – and Quincy often represents better value for money. Pronounced 'KAN-see'.

Quinta – Portuguese for, 'farm', or 'estate'. It precedes the names of many of Portugal's best-known wines. It is pronounced 'KEEN-ta'.

R

racy – Evocative wine-tasting description for wine that thrills the tastebuds with a rush of exciting sensations. Good Rieslings often qualify.

raisiny – Wines from grapes that have been very ripe or overripe at harvest can take on a smell and flavour akin to the concentrated, heat-dried sweetness of raisins. As a minor element in the character of a wine, this can add to the appeal, but as a dominant characteristic it is a fault.

rancio – Spanish term harking back to Roman times when wines were commonly stored in jars outside, exposed to the sun, so they oxidised and took on a burnt sort of flavour. Today, rancio describes a baked – and by no means unpleasant – flavour in fortified wines, particularly sherry and Madeira.

Reserva – In Portugal and Spain, this has genuine significance. The Portuguese use it for special wines with a higher alcohol level and longer ageing, although the precise periods vary between regions. In Spain, especially in the Navarra and Rioja regions, it means the wine must have had at least a year in oak and two in bottle before release.

reserve – On French (as *réserve*) or other wines, this implies special-quality, longer-aged wines, but has no official significance.

Retsina – The universal white wine of Greece. It has been traditionally made in Attica, the region of Athens, for a very long time, and is said to owe its origins and name to the ancient custom of sealing amphorae (terracotta jars) of the wine with a gum made from pine resin. Some of the flavour of the resin inevitably transmitted itself into the wine, and ancient Greeks acquired a lasting taste for it.

Reuilly – AC of Loire Valley, France, for crisp dry whites from Sauvignon grapes. Pronounced 'RER-yee'.

Ribatejo – Emerging wine region of Portugal. Worth seeking out on labels of red wines in particular, because new winemakers are producing lively stuff from distinctive indigenous grapes such as Castelao and Trincadeira.

Ribera del Duero – Classic wine region of north-west Spain lying along the river Duero (which crosses the border to become Portugal's Douro, forming the valley where port comes from). It is home to an estate rather oddly named Vega Sicilia, where red wines of epic quality are made and sold at equally epic prices. Further down the scale, some very good reds are made, too.

Riesling – The noble grape variety of Germany. It is correctly pronounced 'REEZ-ling', not 'RICE-ling'. Once notorious as the grape behind all those boring 'medium' Liebfraumilchs and Niersteiners, this grape has had a bad press. In fact, there has never been much, if any, Riesling in Germany's cheap-and-nasty plonks. But the country's best wines, the so-called Qualitätswein mit Prädikat grades, are made almost exclusively with Riesling. These wines range from crisply fresh and appley styles to extravagantly fruity, honeyed wines from late-harvested grapes. Excellent Riesling wines are also made in Alsace and now in Australia.

Rioja – The principal fine-wine region of Spain, in the country's north-east. The pricier wines are noted for their vanilla-pod richness from long ageing in oak casks. Younger wines, labelled variously *joven* (young) and *sin crianza* (meaning they are without barrel-ageing), are cheaper and can also make relishable drinking.

Ripasso – A particular style of Valpolicella wine. New wine is partially refermented in vats that have been used to make the recioto reds (wines made from semi-dried grapes), thus creating a bigger, smoother (and more alcoholic) version of usually light and pale Valpolicella.

Riserva – In Italy, a wine made only in the best vintages, and allowed longer ageing in cask and bottle.

Rivaner – Alternative name for Germany's Müller-Thurgau grape, the life-blood of Liebfraumilch.

Riverland – Vineyard region to the immediate north of the Barossa Valley of South Australia, extending east into New South Wales.

Roditis – White grape variety of Greece, known for fresh dry whites with decent acidity, often included in the blend for retsina.

rosso – Red wine, Italy.

Rosso Conero – DOC red wine made in the environs of Ancona in the Marches, Italy. Made from the Montepulciano grape, the wine can provide excellent value for money.

Ruby Cabernet – Black grape variety of California, created by crossing Cabernet Sauvignon and Carignan. Makes soft and squelchy red wine at home and in South Africa.

Rueda – DO of north-west Spain making first-class refreshing dry whites from the indigenous Verdejo grape, imported Sauvignon grape, and others. Exciting quality – and prices, so far, are keen.

Rully – AC of Chalonnais region of southern Burgundy, France. White wines from Chardonnay and red wines from Pinot Noir grapes. Both can be very good and are substantially cheaper than their more northerly Burgundian neighbours. Pronounced 'ROO-yee'.

S

Saint Emilion – AC of Bordeaux, France. Centred on the romantic hill town of St Emilion, this famous sub-region makes some of the grandest red wines of France, and also some of the best-value ones. St Emilion lies due east of the city of Bordeaux. It has very different weather and soil conditions from the more famous Médoc, to the north-west of the city, and produces faster-maturing wines, largely from Merlot and Cabernet Franc grapes. Each vintage since 1998 has produced many good wines – and some poor ones, too, it must be said – and most of the bottles to be found in supermarkets will be mature enough to drink now. The grandest wines are classified 1er Grand Cru Classé and are madly expensive, but many more are classified respectively Grand Cru Classé and Grand Cru, and these designations can be seen as a fairly trustworthy indicator of quality. There are several 'satellite' St Emilion ACs named after the villages at their centres, notably Lussac St Emilion, Montagne St Emilion and Puisseguin St Emilion. Some excellent wines are made by estates within these ACs, and at relatively affordable prices thanks to the comparatively humble status of their satellite designations.

Salento – Up-and-coming wine region of southern Italy. Many good bargain reds from local grapes including Nero d'Avola and Primitivo.

Sancerre – AC of the Loire Valley, France, renowned for flinty-fresh Sauvignon whites and rarer Pinot Noir reds. These wines are never cheap, and recent tastings make it plain that only the best-made, individual-producer wines are worth the money. Budget brands seem mostly dull.

Sangiovese – The local black grape of Tuscany, Italy. It is the principal variety used for Chianti and is now widely planted in Latin America – often making delicious, Chianti-like wines with characteristic cherryish-but-deeply-ripe fruit and a dry, clean finish. Chianti wines have become (unjustifiably) expensive in recent years, and cheaper Italian wines such as those called Sangiovese di Toscana make a consoling substitute.

Santorini – Island of Greece's Cyclades was the site in about 1500BC of a tremendous volcanic explosion. The huge caldera of the volcano – a circular mini-archipelago – is now planted with vines producing very trendy and likeable dry white wines at fair prices.

Saumur – Town and appellation of Loire Valley, France. Characterful minerally red wines from Cabernet Franc grapes, and some whites. The once popular sparkling wines from Chenin Blanc grapes are now little seen in Britain.

Saumur-Champigny – Separate appellation for red wines from Cabernet Franc grapes of Saumur in the Loire, sometimes very good and lively.

Sauvignon Blanc – French white grape variety now grown worldwide. The wines are characterised by aromas of gooseberry, fresh-cut grass, even asparagus. Flavours are often described as 'grassy' or 'nettley'.

sec – Dry wine style. French.

secco – Dry wine style. Italian.

Semillon – White grape variety originally of Bordeaux, where it is blended with Sauvignon Blanc to make fresh dry whites and, when harvested very late in the season, the ambrosial sweet whites of Barsac, Sauternes and other appellations. Even in the driest wines, the grape can be recognised from its honeyed, sweet-pineapple, even banana-like aromas. It is now widely planted in Australia and Latin America, and frequently blended with Chardonnay to make interesting dry whites.

sherry – The great aperitif wine of Spain, centred on the Andalusian city of Jerez (of which the name 'sherry' is an English mispronunciation). There is a lot of sherry-style wine in the world, but only the authentic wine from Jerez and the neighbouring producing towns of Puerta de Santa Maria and Sanlucar de Barrameda may label their wines as such. The Spanish drink real sherry – very dry and fresh, pale in colour and served well chilled (called fino and manzanilla), and darker but naturally dry variations called amontillado, palo cortado and oloroso. The stuff sold under the big brand names for the British market are sweetened, coloured commercial yuck for putting in trifles or sideboard decanters to gather dust. The sherries recommended in this book are all real wines, made the way the Spanish like them.

Shiraz – Australian name for the Syrah grape. Aussie Shirazes, unlike their silky-spicy southern French counterparts, tend to be big, muscular and alcoholic wines with earthy darkness.

Sogrape – The leading wine company of Portugal, which built its fortune on Mateus Rosé. Sogrape is based in the Douro region, where port comes from, and makes many excellent table wines both locally and further afield. In 2002, Sogrape added the huge port (and sherry) house of Sandeman to its port-making interests.

Somontano – Wine region of north-east Spain. Name means 'under the mountains' – in this case the Pyrenees – and the region has had DO status only since 1984. Much innovative winemaking here, with New World styles emerging. Some very good buys. A region to watch.

souple – French wine-tasting term that translates into English as 'supple' or even 'docile', as in 'pliable', but I understand it in the vinous context to mean muscular but soft – a wine with tannin as well as soft fruit.

Spätlese – See QmP.

spirity – Some wines, mostly from the New World, are made from grapes so ripe at harvest that their high alcohol content can be detected through a mildly burning sensation on the tongue, similar to the effect of sipping a spirit.

spritzy – Describes a wine with a barely detectable sparkle. Some young wines are intended to have this elusive fizziness; in others it is a fault.

spumante – Sparkling wine of Italy. Asti Spumante is the best known, from the town of Asti in the north-west Italian province of Piemonte. The term describes wines that are fully sparkling. Frizzante wines have a less vigorous mousse.

stalky – A useful tasting term to describe red wines with flavours that make you think the stalks from the grape bunches must have been fermented along with the must (juice). Young Bordeaux reds very often have this mild astringency. In moderation it's fine, but if it dominates it probably signifies the wine is at best immature and at worst badly made.

Stellenbosch – Town and region at the heart of South Africa's burgeoning wine industry. It's an hour's drive from Cape Town and the source of much of the country's cheaper wine. Quality is variable, and the name Stellenbosch on a label can't (yet, anyway) be taken as a guarantee of quality.

stony – Wine-tasting term for keenly dry white wines. It's meant to indicate a wine of purity and real quality, with just the right match of fruit and acidity.

structured – Good wines are not one-dimensional; they have layers of flavour and texture. A structured wine has phases of enjoyment: the 'attack' or first impression in the mouth; the middle palate as the wine is held in the mouth; the lingering aftertaste.

summer fruit – Wine-tasting term intended to convey a smell or taste of soft fruits such as strawberries and raspberries – without having to commit too specifically to which.

Superiore – On labels of Italian wines, this is more than an idle boast. Under DOC rules, wines must qualify for the superiore designation by reaching one or more specified quality levels, usually a higher alcohol content or an additional period of maturation. Frascati, for example, qualifies for DOC status at 11.5% alcohol, but to be classified superiore must have 12% alcohol.

sur lie – Literally, 'on the lees'. It's a term now widely used on the labels of Muscadet wines, signifying that after fermentation has died down, the new wine has been left in the tank over the winter on the lees – the detritus of yeasts and other interesting compounds left over from the turbid fermentation process. The idea is that additional interest is imparted into the flavour of the wine.

Syrah – The noble grape of the Rhône Valley, France. Makes very dark, dense wine characterised by peppery, tarry aromas. Now planted all over southern France and farther afield. In Australia, where it makes wines ranging from disagreeably jam-like plonks to wonderfully rich and silky keeping wines, it is known as Shiraz.

T

table wine – Wine that is unfortified and of an alcoholic strength, for UK tax purposes anyway, of no more than 15%. I use the term to distinguish, for example, between the red table wines of the Douro Valley in Portugal and the region's better-known fortified wine, port.

Tafelwein – Table wine, German. The humblest quality designation, which doesn't usually bode very well.

tank method – Bulk-production process for sparkling wines. Base wine undergoes secondary fermentation in a large, sealed vat rather than in individual closed bottles. Also known as the Charmat method after the name of the inventor of the process.

tannin – Well-known as the film-forming, teeth-coating component in tea, tannin is a natural compound occurring in black grape skins and acts as a natural preservative in wine. Its noticeable presence in wine is regarded as a good thing. It gives young everyday reds their dryness, firmness of flavour and backbone. And it helps high-quality reds to retain their lively fruitiness for many years. A grand Bordeaux red when first made, for example, will have purply-sweet, rich fruit and mouth-puckering tannin, but after a few years this will have evolved into a delectably fruity mature wine in which the formerly parching effects of the tannin have receded almost completely, leaving the shade of 'residual tannin' that marks out a great wine approaching maturity.

tarry – On the whole, winemakers don't like critics to say their wines evoke the redolence of road repairs, but I can't help using this term to describe the agreeable, sweet, 'burnt' flavour that is often found at the centre of the fruit in wines from Argentina, Italy and Portugal in particular.

TCA – Dread ailment in wine blamed on faulty corks. It stands for 246 trichloroanisol and is characterised by a horrible musty smell and flavour in the affected wine. It is largely because of the current plague of TCA that so many wine producers worldwide are now going over to polymer 'corks' and screwcaps.

tears – The colourless alcohol in the wine left clinging to the inside of the glass after the contents have been swirled. Persistent tears (also known as 'legs') indicate a wine of good concentration.

Tempranillo – The great black grape of Spain. Along with Garnacha (Grenache in France), it makes all red Rioja and Navarra wines and, under many pseudonyms, is an important or exclusive contributor to the wines of many other regions of Spain. It is also widely cultivated in South America.

tinto – On Spanish labels indicates a deeply coloured red wine. *Clarete* denotes a paler colour. Also Portuguese.

Toro – Quality wine region east of Zamora, Spain.

Torrontes – White grape variety of Argentina. Makes soft, dry wines often with delicious grapey-spicy aroma, similar in style to the classic dry Muscat wines of Alsace, but at more accessible prices.

Touraine – Region encompassing a swathe of the Loire Valley, France. Non-AC wines may be labelled 'Sauvignon de Touraine' etc.

Touriga Nacional – The most valued black grape variety of the Douro Valley in Portugal, where port is made. The name Touriga now appears on an increasing number of table wines made as sidelines by the port producers. They can be very good, with the same spirity aroma and sleek flavours of port itself, minus the fortification.

Traminer – Grape variety, the same as Gewürztraminer.

Trebbiano – The workhorse white grape of Italy. A productive variety that is easy to cultivate, it seems to be included in just about every well known white wine of the entire nation – including Frascati, Orvieto and Soave. It is the same grape as France's Ugni Blanc. There are, however, distinct regional variations of the grape. Trebbiano di Lugana makes a distinctive white in the DOC of the name, sometimes very good, while Trebbiano di Toscana makes a major contribution to the distinctly less interesting dry whites of Chianti country.

Trincadeira Preta – Portuguese black grape variety native to the port-producing vineyards of the Douro Valley (where it goes under the name Tinta Amarella). In southern Portugal, it produces dark and sturdy table wines.

trocken – 'Dry' German wine. It's a recent trend among commercial-scale producers in the Rhine and Mosel to label their wines with this description in the hope of reassuring consumers that the contents do not resemble the dreaded sugar-water Liebfraumilch-type plonks of the bad old days. But the description does have a particular meaning under German wine law, namely that there is only a low level of unfermented sugar lingering in the wine (9 grams per litre, if you need to know), and this can leave the wine tasting rather austere.

U

Ugni Blanc – The most widely cultivated white grape variety of France and the mainstay of many a cheap dry white wine. To date it has been better known as the provider of base wine for distilling into Armagnac and Cognac, but lately the name has been appearing on wine labels. Technology seems to be improving the performance of the grape. The curious name is pronounced 'OON-yee', and is the same variety as Italy's ubiquitous Trebbiano.

V

Vacqueyras – Village of the southern Rhône valley of France in the region better known for its generic appellation, the Côtes du Rhône. Vacqueyras can date its winemaking history all the way back to 1414, but has only been producing under its own village AC since 1991. The wines, from Grenache and Syrah grapes, can be wonderfully silky and intense, spicy and long-lived.

Valdepeñas – An island of quality production amidst the ocean of mediocrity that is Spain's La Mancha region – where most of the grapes are grown for distilling into the head-banging brandies of Jerez. Valdepeñas reds are made from a grape they call the Cencibel – which turns out to be a very close relation of the Tempranillo grape that is the mainstay of the fine but expensive red wines of Rioja. Again, like Rioja, Valdepeñas wines are matured in oak casks to give them a vanilla-rich smoothness. Among bargain reds, Valdepeñas is a name to look out for.

Valpolicella – Red wine of Verona, Italy. Good examples have ripe cherry fruit and a pleasingly dry finish. Unfortunately, there are many bad examples of Valpolicella. Shop with circumspection. Valpolicella Classico wines, from the best vineyards clustered around the town, are more reliable. Those additionally labelled superiore have higher alcohol and some bottle-age.

vanilla – Ageing wines in oak barrels (or, less picturesquely, adding oak chips to wine in huge concrete vats) imparts a range of characteristics, including a smell of vanilla from the ethyl vanilline naturally given off by oak.

varietal – A varietal wine is one named after the grape variety (one or more) from which it is made. Nearly all everyday wines worldwide are now labelled in this way. It is salutary to contemplate that just 20 years ago, wines described thus were virtually unknown outside Germany and one or two quirky regions of France and Italy.

vegan-friendly – My informal way of noting that a wine is claimed to have been made not only with animal-product-free finings (see Vegetarian wine) but also without any animal-related products whatsoever, such as manure in the vineyards.

vegetal – A tasting note definitely open to interpretation. It suggests a smell or flavour reminiscent less of fruit (apple, pineapple, strawberry and the like) than of something leafy or even root-based. Some wines are evocative (to some tastes) of beetroot, cabbage or even unlikelier vegetable flavours – and these characteristics may add materially to the attraction of the wine.

vegetarian wine – Given that proper wine consists of nothing other than grape juice and the occasional innocent natural additive, it might seem facile to qualify it as a vegetable product. But most wines are 'fined' – clarified – with animal products. These include egg whites, isinglass from fish bladders and casein from milk. Gelatin, a beef by-product, is also used. Consumers who prefer to avoid contact, however remote, with these products, should look out for wines labelled suitable for vegetarians and/or vegans. The wines will have been fined with bentonite, an absorbent clay first found at Benton in the US state of Montana.

Verdejo – White grape of the Rueda region in NW Spain. It can make superbly perfumed crisp dry whites of truly distinctive character and has helped make Rueda one of the best white wine sources of Europe. No relation to Verdelho.

Verdelho – Portuguese grape variety once mainly used for a medium-dry style of Madeira, also called Verdelho, but now rare. The vine is now prospering in Australia, where it can make well balanced dry whites with fleeting richness and lemon-lime acidity.

Verdicchio – White grape variety of Italy best known in the DOC zone of Castelli dei Jesi in the Adriatic wine region of the Marches. Dry white wines once known for little more than their naff amphora-style bottles but now gaining a reputation for interesting, herbaceous flavours of recognisable character.

Vermentino – White grape variety principally of Italy, especially Sardinia. Makes florally scented, soft dry whites.

Vin Délimité de Qualité Supérieur – Usually abbreviated to VDQS, a French wine quality designation between appellation contrôlée and vin de pays. To qualify, the wine has to be from approved grape varieties grown in a defined zone. This designation is gradually disappearing.

vin de liqueur – Sweet style of white wine mostly from the Pyrenean region of south-westernmost France, made by adding a little spirit to the new wine before it has fermented out, halting the fermentation and retaining sugar.

vin de pays – 'Country wine' of France. The French map is divided up into more than 100 vin de pays regions. Wine in bottles labelled as such must be from grapes grown in the nominated zone or département. Some vin de pays areas are huge: the Vin de Pays d'Oc (named after the Languedoc region) covers much of the Midi and Provence. Plenty of wines bearing this humble designation are of astoundingly high quality and certainly compete with New World counterparts for interest and value.

Vin de Pays Catalan – Zone of sub-Pyrenees region (Roussillon) of south-west France.

Vin de Pays de L'Hérault – Zone within Languedoc-Roussillon region of south-west France.

Vin de Pays des Coteaux du Luberon – Zone of Provence, France.

Vin de Pays des Côtes de Gascogne – Zone of 'Gascony' region in south-west France.

Vin de Pays de Vaucluse – Zone of southern Rhône Valley.

Vin de Pays d'Oc – Largest of the zones, encompasses much of the huge region of the Languedoc, of south-west France. Many excellent wines are sold under this classification, particularly those made in appellation areas from grapes not permitted locally.

Vin de Pays du Gers – Zone of south-west France including Gascony. White wines principally from Ugni Blanc and Colombard grapes.

Vin de Pays du Jardin de la France – Zone of the Loire Valley.

vin de table – The humblest official classification of French wine. Neither the region, grape varieties nor vintage need be stated on the label. The wine might not even be French. Don't expect too much from this kind of 'table wine'.

vin doux – Sweet, mildly fortified wine mostly of France, usually labelled vin doux naturel. A little spirit is added during the winemaking process, halting the fermentation by killing the yeast before it has consumed all the sugars – thus the pronounced sweetness of the wine.

vin gris – Rosé wine from Provence. They call it gris ('grey') because it's halfway between red (the new black, you might say) and white.

Vinho de mesa – 'Table wine' of Portugal.

Vino da tavola – The humblest official classification of Italian wine. Much ordinary plonk bears this designation, but the bizarre quirks of Italy's wine laws dictate that some of that country's finest wines are also classed as mere vino da tavola (table wine). If an expensive Italian wine is labelled as such, it doesn't mean it will be a disappointment.

Vino de mesa – 'Table wine' of Spain. Usually very ordinary.

vintage – The grape harvest. The year displayed on bottle labels is the year of the harvest. Wines bearing no date have been blended from the harvests of two or more years.

Viognier – A grape variety once exclusive to the northern Rhône Valley in France, where it makes a very chi-chi wine, Condrieu, usually costing £20-plus. Now, the Viognier is grown more widely, in North and South America as well as elsewhere in France, and occasionally produces soft, marrowy whites that echo the grand style of Condrieu itself.

Viura – White grape variety of Rioja, Spain. Also widely grown elsewhere in Spain under the name Macabeo. Wines have a blossomy aroma and are dry, but sometimes soft at the expense of acidity.

Vouvray – AC of the Loire Valley, France, known for still and sparkling dry white wines and sweet, still whites from late-harvested grapes. The wines, all from Chenin Blanc grapes, have a unique capacity for unctuous softness combined with lively freshness – an effect best portrayed in the demi-sec (slightly sweet) wines, which can be delicious and keenly priced. Unfashionable, but worth looking out for.

W

weight – In an ideal world the weight of a wine is determined by the ripeness of the grapes from which it has been made. In some cases the weight is determined merely by the quantity of sugar added during the production process. A good, genuine wine described as having weight is one in which there is plenty of alcohol and 'extract' – colour and flavour from the grapes. Wine enthusiasts judge weight by swirling the wine in the glass and then examining the 'legs' or 'tears' left clinging to the inside of the glass after the contents have subsided. Alcohol gives these runlets a dense, glycerine-like condition, and if they cling for a long time, the wine is deemed to have weight – a very good thing in all honestly made wines.

Winzergenossenschaft – One of the many very lengthy and peculiar words regularly found on labels of German wines. This means a winemaking co-operative. Many excellent German wines are made by these associations of growers.

woodsap – A subjective tasting note. Some wines have a fleeting bitterness, which is not a fault, but an interesting balancing factor amidst very ripe flavours. The effect somehow evokes woodsap.

X

Xarel-lo – One of the main grape varieties for cava, the sparkling wine of Spain.

Xinomavro – Black grape variety of Greece. It retains its acidity even in the very hot conditions that prevail in many Greek vineyards – where harvests tend to overripen and make cooked-tasting wines. Modern winemaking techniques are capable of making well balanced wines from Xinomavro.

Y

Yecla – Town and DO wine region of eastern Spain, close to Alicante, making lots of interesting, strong-flavoured red and white wines, often at bargain prices.

yellow – White wines are not white at all, but various shades of yellow – or, more poetically, gold. Some white wines with opulent richness even have a flavour I cannot resist calling 'yellow' – reminiscent of butter.

Z

Zefir – Hungarian white grape variety that can (on a good day) produce a spicy, dry wine rather like the Gewürztraminer of Alsace.

Zenit – Hungarian white grape variety. Produces dry wines.

Zinfandel – Black grape variety of California. Makes brambly reds, some of which can age very gracefully, and 'blush' whites – actually pink, because a little of the skin colour is allowed to leach into the must. The vine is also planted in Australia and South America. The Primitivo of southern Italy is said to be a related variety, but makes a very different kind of wine.

Wine Rituals

There has always been a lot of nonsense talked about the correct ways to serve wine. Red wine, we are told, should be opened and allowed to 'breathe' before pouring. White wine should be chilled. Wine doesn't go with soup, tomatoes or chocolate. You know the sort of thing.

It would all be simply laughable, except that these daft conventions do make so many potential wine lovers nervous about the simple ritual of opening a bottle and sharing it around. Here is a short and opinionated guide to the received wisdom of wine serving.

Breathing

Simply uncorking a wine for an hour or two before you serve it will make absolutely no difference to the way it tastes. However, if you wish to warm up an icy bottle of red by placing it near (never on) a radiator or fire, do remove the cork first. As the wine warms, even very slightly, it gives off gas, which will spoil the flavour if it cannot escape.

Chambré-ing

One of the more florid terms in the wine vocabulary. The idea is that red wine should be at the same temperature as the room (*chambre*) you're going to drink it in. In fairness, it makes sense – although the term harks back to the days when the only people who drank wine were those who could afford to keep it in the freezing-cold vaulted cellars beneath their houses. The ridiculously high temperatures to which some homes are raised by central heating systems today are really far too warm for wine. But presumably those who live in such circumstances do so out of choice, and will prefer their wine to be similarly overheated.

Chilling

Drink your white wine as cold as you like. It's certainly true that good whites are at their best at a cool rather than at an icy temperature, but cheap and characterless wines can be improved immeasurably if they are cold enough – the anaesthetising effect of the temperature removes all sense of taste.

Pay no attention to notions that red wine should not be served cool. There are plenty of lightweight reds that will respond very well to an hour in the fridge.

Corked wine

Wine trade surveys reveal that far too many bottles are in no fit state to be sold. The villain is very often cited as the cork. Cut from the bark of cork-oak trees cultivated for the purpose in Portugal and Spain, these natural stoppers have done sterling service for 200 years but now face a crisis of confidence among wine producers. A diseased or damaged cork can make the wine taste stale because air has penetrated, or musty-mushroomy due to a chemical reaction. These faults in wine, known as 'corked' or 'corky', should be immediately obvious, even in the humblest bottle, and you should return the bottle to the supplier and demand a refund. A warning here. Bad corks tend to come in batches. It might be wise not to accept another bottle of the same wine but to choose something else.

Today, many wine producers are opting to close their bottles with polymer bungs. Some are designed to resemble the 'real thing' while others come in a rather disorienting range of colours – including black. There seems to be no evidence that these synthetic products do any harm to the wine, but it might not be sensible to 'lay down' bottles closed with polymer. The effects of years of contact with these materials are yet to be scientifically established. All of this applies equally to the screwcap closures now replacing corks.

Corkscrews

The best kind of corkscrew is the 'waiter's friend' type. It looks like a pen-knife, unfolding a 'worm' (the helix or screw) and a lever device which, after the worm has been driven into the cork (try to centre it) rests on the lip of the bottle and enables you to withdraw the cork with minimal effort. These devices are cheaper and longer-lasting than any of the more elaborate types, and are equally effective at withdrawing the new polymer bungs – which can be hellishly difficult to unwind from Teflon-coated 'continuous' corkscrews such as the Screwpull.

Decanting

There are two views on the merits of decanting wines. The prevailing one seems to be that it is pointless and even pretentious. The other is that it can make real improvements in the way a wine tastes and is definitely worth the trouble.

Of course, it's all too easy to drift into the dangerous realms of pretentiousness here, but there's nothing like a real experiment to keep minds concentrated on the facts. Scientists, not usually much exercised by the finer nuances of wine, will tell you that exposure to the air causes wine to 'oxidise' – take in oxygen molecules that will quite quickly initiate the process of turning wine into vinegar – and anyone who has tasted a 'morning-after' glass of wine will no doubt vouch for this.

But the fact that wine does oxidise is a real clue to the reality of the effects of exposure to air. Shut inside its bottle, a young wine is very much a live substance, jumping with natural, but mysterious, compounds that can cause all sorts of strange taste sensations. But by exposing the wine to air these effects are markedly reduced.

In wines that spend longer in the bottle, the influence of these factors diminishes, in a process called 'reduction'. In red wines, the hardness of tannin – the natural preservative imparted into wine from the grape skins – gradually reduces, just as the raw purple colour darkens to ruby and later to orangey-brown.

I believe there is less reason for decanting old wines than new, unless the old wine has thrown a deposit and needs carefully to be poured off it. And in some light-bodied wines, such as older Rioja, decanting is probably a bad idea, because it can accelerate oxidation all too quickly.

As to actual experiments, I have carried out several of my own with wines opened in advance or wines decanted compared to the same wines just opened and poured, and my own unscientific judgement is that big, young, alcoholic reds can certainly be improved by aeration. So I was pleased to read about two distinguished doctors who recently carried out a revealing experiment of their own in the hope of proving once and for all whether there is any point in opening a bottle of red wine in advance.

Dr Nirmal Charan is a pulmonologist (lung specialist) of Boise, Idaho, USA. Dr Pier Giuseppe Agostoni is a cardiologist from the University of Milan in Italy. Their experiment was intended to resolve a good-natured disagreement that arose between them over the dinner table at Dr Charan's home in Idaho. The host suggested to Dr Agostino that he might like to try a bottle of Idaho wine. Dr A assented but suggested to Dr C that it would be a good idea to open the bottle an hour or so in advance to let it breathe.

As a consultant in pulmonary medicine and something of an expert in matters of respiration, Dr C pointed out to his guest that there was no scientific basis for the suggested course of action. In the proper spirit of empiricism, the two agreed that the dispute should be settled by a controlled test.

And so the following day the learned pair adjourned to Dr C's laboratory at the VA Medical Center in Boise, armed with five bottles of Cabernet Sauvignon. The cork of each bottle was penetrated with a hypodermic needle and a small sample of wine taken. Each was measured for oxygen pressure in an arterial blood gas analyser, giving the reading of 30 ml of mercury (as compared to 90 ml in well-oxygenated human blood).

Next, the wines were opened. Further samples were taken after periods of two, four, six and 24 hours. For the first periods, the reading remained unaltered. Only after 24 hours had it increased significantly – to 61 ml.

Meanwhile, the doctors tried pouring samples from another bottle of the wine into glasses and swirling it round. After only a couple of minutes, the reading reached 150 ml.

Dr Agostoni was impressed. He returned to Milan and put his new-found wisdom to the test by inviting 35 friends to a party. He gave them all wine that had been swirled, and then wine that had been newly opened. Only two among the throng acknowledged no difference.

Then Dr A gave the guests a 'blind' tasting of swirled and unswirled wines. To his considerable satisfaction, all but one were able to tell the difference, and agreed the wine tasted significantly better with aeration.

Dr A passed these results on to his friend back in Idaho. The grateful Dr Charan was able to incorporate the information into a sideshow presentation at that year's meeting of the American Lung Association in Chicago. 'Just like blood,' Dr C told an enthralled audience of pulmonologists and thoracic surgeons, 'oxygenated wine is better than non-oxygenated wine.'

Glasses

Does it make any difference whether you drink your wine from a hand-blown crystal glass or a plastic cup? Do experiment! Conventional wisdom suggests that the ideal glass is clear, uncut, long-stemmed and with a tulip-shaped bowl large enough to hold a generous quantity when filled only halfway up. The idea is that you can hold the glass by its stalk rather than by its bowl. This gives an uninterrupted view of the colour, and prevents you smearing the bowl with your sticky fingers. By filling the glass only halfway up, you give the wine a chance to 'bloom', showing off its wonderful perfume. You can then intrude your nose into the air space within the glass, without getting it wet, to savour the bouquet. It's all harmless fun, really – and quite difficult to perform if the glass is an undersized Paris goblet filled, like a pub measure, to the brim.

Washing glasses

If your wine glasses are of any value to you, don't put them in the dishwasher. Over time, they'll craze from the heat of the water. And they will not emerge in the glitteringly pristine condition suggested by the pictures on some detergent packets. For genuinely perfect glasses that will stay that way, wash them in hot soapy water, rinse with clean, hot water and dry immediately with a glass cloth kept exclusively for this purpose. Sounds like fanaticism, but if you take your wine seriously, you'll see there is sense in it.

Keeping wine

How long can you keep an opened bottle of wine before it goes downhill? Not long. A re-corked bottle with just a glassful out of it should stay fresh until the day after, but if there is a lot of air inside the bottle, the wine will oxidise, turning progressively stale and sour. Wine 'saving' devices that allow you to withdraw the air from the bottle via a punctured, self-sealing rubber stopper are variably effective, but don't expect these to keep a wine fresh for more than a couple of re-openings. A crafty method of keeping a half-finished bottle is to decant it, via a funnel, into a clean half bottle and recork.

Storing wine

Supermarket labels always seem to advise that 'this wine should be consumed within one year of purchase'. I think this is a wheeze to persuade customers to drink it up quickly and come back for more. Many of the more robust red wines are likely to stay in good condition for much more than one year, and plenty will actually improve with age. On the other hand, it is a sensible axiom that inexpensive dry white wines are better the younger they are. If you do intend to store wines for longer than a few weeks, do pay heed to the conventional wisdom that bottles are best stored in low, stable temperatures, preferably in the dark. Bottles closed with conventional corks should be laid on their side lest the corks dry out for lack of contact with the wine. But one of the notable advantages of the new closures now proliferating is that if your wine comes with a polymer 'cork' or a screwcap, you can safely store it upright.

Wine and Food

Wine is made to be drunk with food, but some wines go better with particular dishes than others. It is no coincidence that Italian wines, characterised by soft, cherry fruit and a clean, mouth-drying finish, go so well with the sticky delights of pasta.

But it's personal taste rather than national associations that should determine the choice of wine with food. And if you prefer a black-hearted Argentinian Malbec to a brambly Italian Barbera with your Bolognese, that's fine.

The conventions that have grown up around wine and food pairings do make some sense, just the same. I was thrilled to learn in the early days of my drinking career that sweet, dessert wines can go well with strong blue cheese. As I don't much like puddings but love sweet wines, I was eager to test this match – and I'm here to tell you that it works very well indeed as the end-piece to a grand meal in which there is cheese as well as pud on offer.

Red wine and cheese are supposed to be a natural match, but I'm not so sure. Reds can taste awfully tinny with soft cheeses such as Brie and Camembert, and even worse with goat's cheese. A really extravagant, yellow Australian Chardonnay will make a better match. Hard cheeses such as Cheddar and the wonderful Old Amsterdam (top-of-the-market Gouda) are better with reds.

And then there's the delicate issue of fish. Red wine is supposed to be a no-no. This might well be true of grilled and wholly unadorned white fish, such as sole or a delicate dish of prawns, scallops or crab. But what about oven-roasted monkfish or a substantial winter-season fish pie? An edgy red will do very well indeed, and provide much comfort for those many among us who simply prefer to drink red wine with food, and white wine on its own.

It is very often the method by which dishes are prepared, rather than their core ingredients, that determines which wine will work best. To be didactic, I would always choose Beaujolais or summer-fruit-style reds such as those from Pinot Noir grapes to go with a simple roast chicken. But if the bird is cooked as coq au vin with a hefty wine sauce, I would plump for a much more assertive red.

Some sauces, it is alleged, will overwhelm all wines. Salsa and curry come to mind. I have carried out a number of experiments into this great issue of our time, in my capacity as consultant to a company that specialises in supplying wines to Asian restaurants. One discovery I have made is that forcefully fruity dry white wines with keen acidity can go very well indeed even with fairly incendiary dishes. Sauvignon Blanc with Madras? Give it a try!

I'm also convinced, however, that some red wines will stand up very well to a bit of heat. The marvellously robust Argentinian reds that get such frequent mentions in this book are good partners to Mexican chilli-hot recipes and salsa dishes. The dry, tannic edge to these wines provides a good counterpoint to the inflammatory spices in the food.

Some foods are supposedly impossible to match with wine. Eggs and chocolate are among the prime offenders. And yet, legendary cook Elizabeth David's best-selling autobiography was entitled *An Omelette and a Glass of Wine*, and the affiliation between chocolates and champagne is an unbreakable one. Taste is, after all, that most personally governed of all senses. If your choice is a boiled egg washed down with a glass of claret, who is to say otherwise?

Index